THE SIMON & SCHUSTER
GUIDE TO

CLIMBING PLANTS

FRANCESCA CONSOLINO
ENRICO BANFI

A Fireside Book
Published by Simon & Schuster Inc.
New York London Toronto Sydney Tokyo Singapore

Fireside
Simon & Schuster Inc.
Rockefeller Center
1230 Avenue of the Americas
New York, New York 10020

Art Director: Giorgio Seppi
Drawings by: Giorgio Orlandi
Produced by O.A.F. s.r.l., Milan

Printed and bound in Spain by Artes Gráficas Toledo

D.L.TO:1015–1994

10 9 8 7 6 5 4 3 2 1

Library of Congress Cataloging in Publication Data

Consolino, Francesca.
    The Simon & Schuster guide to climbing plants/Francesca
Consolino, Enrico Banfi: [translated by John Gilbert].
        p.   cm.
    "A Fireside book."
    Includes bibliographical references (p.   ) and index.
    ISBN 0-671-51050-9
    1. Ornamental climbing plants.   I. Banff, Enrico.   II. Title.
III. Title: Simon and Schuster guide to climbing plants.   IV. Title:
Guide to climbing plants.
S8427.C66   1994
635.9′74—dc20
                                                            94-32069
                                                            CIP

CONTENTS

NOTE

The 152 illustrated entries in this book are arranged in natural, that is, systematic sequence. Had the book been designed for specific purposes of identification, other criteria (based on alphabetical order, flower color, type of use, and so on) might have been adopted, but it has seemed more correct to adhere to the natural ties of relationship among the species of the climbing plants under discussion. The sequence of entries, therefore, as well as the names of orders and families, follow the classifications of Pichi Sermolli in respect of ferns (*Lygodium flexuosum*), of Cronquist for dicotyledons (*Magnoliopsida*), and of Dahlgren, Clifford, and Yeo for monocotyledons (*Liliopsida*).

Each entry comprises ten headings. The first, the title, is the **Scientific Name** of the species, including **Synonyms** where these are commonly accepted. The **Common Name** in English is given if in current usage. Then follow the names of the **Order** and the **Family**. **Origin** refers to the climber's country of origin (i.e. the natural wild stock); where the origin is allotopical, for example by hybridization between species from different geographical areas or from cultivars, such an origin is indicated without geographical reference. The sixth heading, **Description**, provides a concise account of the plant's morphology. The seventh is **Flowering Period**, referring as nearly as possible to "normal" conditions, for example, in the open, in a temperate climate. Under **Cultivation** are listed notes and suggestions as to how, when, and where to grow the plant. **Propagation** contains tips on the techniques and best times for reproducing the climber. And the tenth and last heading, **Use**, gives information on the behavior of the species in nature and suggests various possible uses for it.

In the case of certain entries, under **Varieties**, there is a list of the principal and most interesting cultivated varieties of that species.

KEY TO SYMBOLS

outdoor plant

indoor plant

climbing plant with
persistent leaves

climbing plant with
deciduous leaves

decorative plant
for fruits

decorative plant
for leaves

decorative plant
for flowers

plant used for smooth
surfaces, walls, and columns

plant used for
trellises and pergolas

GENERAL INFORMATION

What is a climbing plant? A practical definition would be a plant which, to all intents and purposes, is rooted in the ground and whose development depends on making contact, by whatever means possible, with a support. Such a precise description rules out plants such as the ivy-leaved pelargonium (*Pelargonium peltatum*), the *Aeschynanthus* and *Drosanthemum* genera, the spiderworts (*Tradescantia* spp), and so on, which develop long, soft, hanging or creeping stems, but which, in fact, are not climbers. Most climbing plants will adopt a creeping habit if they do not find a support to which they can adhere; some rain forest lianas, for example, may creep several dozen or hundred yards along the ground. During a summer walk in the country, one may sometimes see spectacular white blooms of the field bindweed (*Convolvulus arvensis*), a typical climbing species with soft, slender stems carpeting the edges of farmland and lanes. Broadly speaking, therefore, all climbers may appear as creepers, but not all creepers are necessarily climbers.

Likewise excluded from our general definition are two further plant categories: *epiphytes* and *parasites*. Epiphytes, with a predominantly tropical distribution, often lack a normal root apparatus and live on branches or trunks of trees, on rocks or on walls, seeking the light and sometimes, as in the case of *Tillandsia usneoides*, developing a system of spidery, drooping stems. These can hardly be mistaken for climbers, for, unlike the latter, they are plants whose seeds, principally transported by birds, germinate in the ground, and which grow already attached to their support. Rather less clear-cut is the distinction between climbers and *hemiparasites*, which cling to the trunks and branches of trees (as, for example, many tropical species of *Loranthus*), covering them with their green leaves so that they sometimes even simulate the foliage of the host itself. Hemiparasites do not have proper roots to connect them directly with the ground but they but do contain chlorophyll, taking in water and mineral salts from the stems of the host plant, into whose tissues they introduce special organs (*haustoria*) that function as suckers. Other plants with climbing habits include the dodders, which are parasites in the fullest sense: they do not contain chlorophyll and depend wholly, and not only for water, on the host plant, clinging tightly to it with their tangle of thin, yellowish caulicles. These species have an interest in keeping the parasitized plant alive, for their own survival depends on it. On the other hand, true climbers, which are not parasites, may even suffocate and kill a host plant used as a support on which to grow: the strangler figs (*Ficus*) of tropical forests and, in temperate climes, the ivy and the clematis, are obvious examples of this.

To conclude, the climbers that form the subject of this book are plants furnished with markedly competitive tendencies and which, in optimal conditions, display an aggressive, luxuriant pattern of growth. This helps to make them both easy and profitable to cultivate.

Why certain plants form a climbing habit

The inexhaustible diversity of modern plant forms is the result of a slow, widespread process that has been continuing ever since life on our planet began. Biological evolution was described by Charles Darwin, who demonstrated how organisms, through their descendants, are subject to a measure of accidental variability and how natural selection favors those individuals who are best prepared to face the problems of survival, at the expense of those less

Above: a Convolvulus, *a typical climbing plant; right: a pendulous plant in a pot.*

11

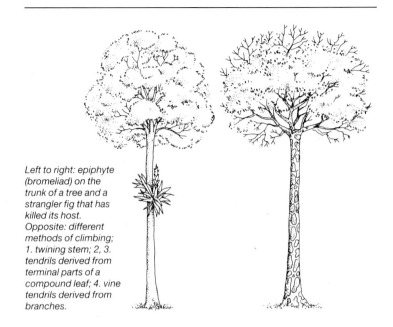

Left to right: epiphyte (bromeliad) on the trunk of a tree and a strangler fig that has killed its host. Opposite: different methods of climbing; 1. twining stem; 2, 3. tendrils derived from terminal parts of a compound leaf; 4. vine tendrils derived from branches.

prepared (hence the familiar saying, "survival of the fittest").

Among the most important requisites of plant survival are space and light. Because in nature individual plants compete for the same environmental resources, their reciprocal struggle for space and light becomes a scenario for natural selection. It is hardly surprising, therefore, that in the course of 120 million years of development, the common flowering plants known as angiosperms have produced the vastest range of adaptations in the entire vegetable kingdom. Without such striking diversification, the rain forest, meadow, swamp, and taiga, to mention only a few examples, would never have taken on their complex and wholly distinctive structures, enabling a very large number of species to share a limited amount of space. In this context the evolutionary advantages of the climbing habit are equally evident. A climber can squeeze its way into the smallest of spaces amid dense vegetation, exhibiting flexibility of growth both upward and sideways, according to its need for light; since it observes no rigid geometrical pattern, unlike a tree or a shrub, it possesses no defined form, adapting itself perfectly to the space available. This explains why the climbing habit has proved so enormously successful in terms of selection, particularly in the forest environment, and why it is so widely represented among groups of angiosperms that differ considerably from one another.

The climbing habit: adaptations and solutions

Comparison of a sufficiently large number of climbing species will reveal that the process of climbing is made possible by virtue of an astonishing variety of anatomical and morphological adaptations. Even so, it is equally evident that this variety can be compressed into a limited range of generalized and fairly repetitive patterns.

First and foremost, the climbing character of a plant is never exhibited during

the early phases that follow seed germination. The plantule of a climbing species is in every way similar to that of a nonclimbing one, at least until the second or third internode begins to lengthen, and sometimes even later. At this point subsequent growth may proceed in different ways depending on whether the plant in question has the propensity to climb by *twining, clinging,* or *scrambling.*

a) *Twiners.* These are climbers whose stems, initially straight, tend to spiral upward around a support, usually from left to right, or clockwise. So the plant adheres firmly to the support by means of its lengthening, twisting main and/or secondary stems. This is one of the least specialized and most common patterns of growth among the climbers, typical, for example, of the morning glory, honeysuckle, and wisteria.

Other climbers within this category are those that twine not only by means of the main stem but also thanks to lateral appendages. In some the leaves or parts of leaves are transformed into appropriate adhesive organs known as *tendrils,* slender but tough threads that corkscrew themselves around the support: this is characteristic of the woody climbers (*Pisum, Vicia, Lathyrus,* and so on) and of many other families. Among the Cucurbitaceae and Passifloraceae the tendrils stem from the leaf axil and can be seen as modified branches. The tendrils of the Vitaceae, likewise transformed branches, may become woody, when they are known as *vine tendrils;* in the genera *Ampelopsis* and *Parthenocissus* they are ramified and end in hooks or in flattened adhesive pads. Elsewhere the tendrils stem from modifications of entire inflorescences, as in the case of the balloon vine (*Cardiospermum halicacabum*). These structures enable the climber to cling to any flat, smooth support such as a rock, wall, or even glass or plastic, enabling it to grow freely and independently.

b) *Clingers.* These climbers do not use the twining pattern but develop special

13

Above and right: ivy with characteristic clinging roots. Opposite, left to right: hooked thorns of a blackberry, climbing palm (Calamus) entangled in the crown of a tree, Smilax aspera *furnished with thorns and tendrils.*

organs that make them capable of clinging more or less firmly to their support. This they achieve by either of two basic methods: by producing *clinging roots* (belonging to the broader category of aerial roots) or by producing thorns or *hooks*.

The former include plants such as the ivy and the creeping fig (*Ficus pumila*), whose stems throw out a very large number of clinging roots which probe into the fissures of bark, wall, or virtually any surface. These roots are often defined as *a*dventitious, but it must be emphasized that true adventitious roots are the exclusive characteristic of monocotyledons (class Liliopsida) which have nothing to do with climbing plants: they are in fact normal roots that are thrown out underground by the seedling in place of the original root which aborts completely in the earliest stages of seed germination.

The second, very widespread, group of clinging climbers affix themselves by means of outgrowths such as spines, hooks, curved bristles, and retrorse (backward-turned) thorns. They often grow most effectively in hedges and areas of scrub and undergrowth where they can look to the support of other plants such as shrubs; because of their relatively stiff stems they are generally capable of supporting themselves more effectively than other climbers. They tend to droop rather than twist, although some of the climbing palms of the genera *Calamus* and *Daemonorops* include veritable spiny lianas which can render vast tracts of rain forest, such as those found in Borneo, virtually impenetrable. Certain thorny climbers with a clinging habit are also furnished with twining tendrils, for example the prickly false-ivy (*Smilax aspera*), a native of the Mediterranean scrubland which clings tenaciously to bushy branches and foliage. Many herbaceous plants have stiff, pointed, curved hairs, or hooks, which also have an adhesive function; among these, although of no interest for

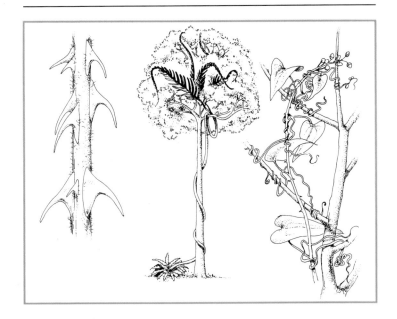

cultivation purposes, is the very common goose-grass or cleavers (*Galium aparine*). Hooks, however, are a less efficient method of adhesion than those previously described.

c) *Scramblers*. These plants are not, strictly speaking, climbers although some, such as the common jasmine (*Jasminum officinale*), have a partially twining habit. In order to grow they must rely on a support but their foliage, instead of clinging to it, scrambles and generally droops over it. Many varieties of so-called climbing roses with this habit are described more accurately as ramblers.

The categories of climbers described so far do not cover the entire range of possibilities and adaptations that exist in nature; nor would there be any point in listing them comprehensively in a book designed primarily for practical reference. Nevertheless it is interesting to note that the standard classifications of climbers, which we have adopted here, deliberately over-simplify reality. Climbing plants very often exhibit two or more different attributes simultaneously, as in the case of the prickly false-ivy, and even more frequently there is no clear-cut boundary between them, any more than there is between the climbing and the "normal" growth habit. It is therefore difficult to attempt an exhaustive survey of the varieties of climbing plants without getting lost in a wealth of misleading and fruitless detail.

Woody and herbaceous climbers
As in virtually all groups of plants, climbers comprise species with thick, woody stems and species with thin, fragile stems. These are extremes, in between which there are all manner of intermediate stages. Woody growth, which is generally regarded as being more primitive, in the evolutionary scale, than

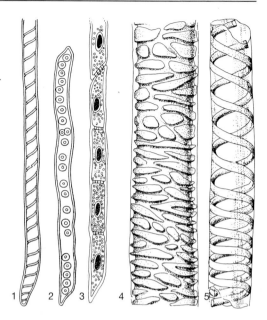

Left to right: 1. tracheids; 2. fibrotracheilds; 3. cells of wood parenchyma; 4. reticulated vessel; 5. double spiralled vessel.

1   2   3   4   5

herbaceous growth, involves so-called secondary growth of the axes (stem and branches). At this point it is worth taking a brief look at the physiology and anatomy of plants in general.

The stems and branches of plants constitute what is called the *cauline apparatus*, which serves to connect the leaves and the soil. Vegetable nutrition or assimilation, which is achieved through photosynthesis, is fundamentally carried out by the leaves: the latter, thanks to the energy source of light, transform water and carbon dioxide into simple sugar (glucose) which is diffused to all the cells of the organism. Supplied through the roots with mineral salts that are dissolved in the ground water, the plant metabolizes the original glucose, transforming it into molecules essential for the life of its own cells: amino acids, proteins, nucleic acids, starch, cellulose, lignin, and so on. This explains the importance of the cauline apparatus in guaranteeing the transport of water and mineral salts from the roots to the leaves, and, similarly, of glucose and its derivatives from the leaves to the roots. The axes are thus formed of tissues specialized in carrying liquids (conducting tissues) and tissues with the function of protection, support, storage, oxygenation, and connection of cells.

In herbaceous axes, which are characteristic of the young caulicles of woody plants, of young spring twigs of trees and shrubs, and of typical grasses, the conducting tissue is situated inside a limited number of *conducting bundles*. These bundles, true organs of transport, are made up, among other things, of supporting tissues (*fibers*) and storage tissues (*parenchyma*). The conducting tissue proper is represented by *tracheids* and *vessels*, which are long, articulated tubes designed to convey water to the leaves, and also by *sieve tubes* necessary for carrying lymph, the water containing the products of photosynthesis, from the leaves to all the living tissues of the plant. While the

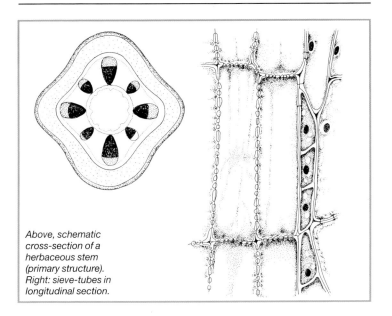

Above, schematic cross-section of a herbaceous stem (primary structure). Right: sieve-tubes in longitudinal section.

sieve tubes have walls of cellulose that are soft and thin, the tracheids and vessels have walls that are variously lignified and are thus fairly stiff and durable. The hardness and thickness of the herbaceous stems is mainly due to a particular supporting tissue *(collenchyma)* which forms a more or less interrupted ring around the inner periphery of the axis, directly beneath the *epidermis*, which constitutes the outer covering.

All of this makes up the so-called *primary structure*. In plants susceptible to further growth, however, the axes develop into a *secondary structure*. This entails an increase in the diameter of the axis, which differs completely from the primary structure. There are no longer any conducting bundles, but rather a single inner mass comprised of tracheids, vessels, fibers, and parenchymas which constitutes the *wood*, in the true sense of the term. The sieve tubes which, with a certain amount of fiber and parenchyma, make up the *liber*, form a thin ring on the periphery; in addition there are other tissues, the outermost of which, *cork*, is the fundamental protective layer. As it thickens and splits on the outside, the cork forms what is commonly called the *bark*. The peripheral tissues are connected radially with the central tissues of the trunk by *medullary* or *pith rays*, which are like vertical strips of parenchyma. The particular nature of the secondary structure enables the stems and branches to grow each year in diameter by the production of new wood toward the outside, to coincide with the construction of a new, substitute peripheral ring of liber, broader than that of the previous year, and, naturally, of new cork on the outside. The characteristic rings visible in the cross-section of a trunk correspond to a favorable growth season, which in temperate and cold climes occurs every year in spring or summer but which in hot climates may be repeated more than once in the same year.

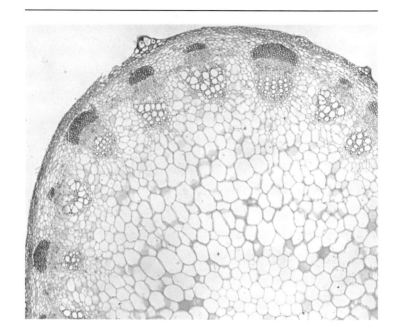

If the transport of liquids requires considerable efficiency on the part of the trunk and branches of, say, an oak, such efficiency must obviously be that much greater in the case, say, of the stem of a liana or a climber. This can be verified by examining the conducting tissue of a climbing plant. The conducting elements of the wood are, as we have seen, the tracheids and vessels: the difference between the two is that whereas the tracheids exhibit transverse septs, although variously perforated to correspond with two superposed joints, the vessels lack these completely and are larger, guaranteeing swifter and more thorough conduction.

The wood of climbers is therefore characterized by a far greater number of vessels than tracheids, made necessary by the incredible length of their stems.

Leaves: function, types, and adaptations
The plant's nutritional system depends on its leaves. From the evolutionary point of view, the leaf is both the oldest and most tested organ of the vegetable kingdom. Yet despite the enormous complexity of the leaf's internal physical/chemical mechanism, its actual structure is relatively simple, comprising very few tissues. The leaf surfaces are covered by a protective, waterproof epidermis, structured in such a way, however, to let through light and to allow the exchange of gases between the inner parts and the atmosphere. The leaf is therefore transparent and provided with adjustable pores called *stomata*. Inside is the *chlorenchyma*, the basic tissue whose cells are responsible for photosynthesis; these cells are filled with *chloroplasts*, mobile organelles of disklike form which are normally golden green in color. Their highly complex structure comprises molecules of chlorophyll and other pigments convert part of the energy of solar radiation into biochemical energy that brings about photosyn-

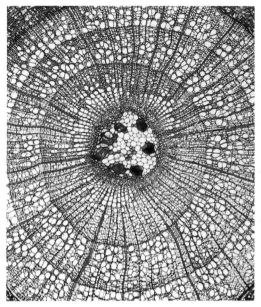

Right: microphotograph of section of a woody stem (secondary structure). Below: section of a leaf, based on thickness: the visible parts are the upper cutinized epidermis, the palisade parenchyma, the lacunulose parenchyma with a conducting bundle, and the lower epidermis with stomata. Opposite: microphotograph of the section of a herbaceous stem in the process of lignifying (intermediate stage between primary and secondary structure).

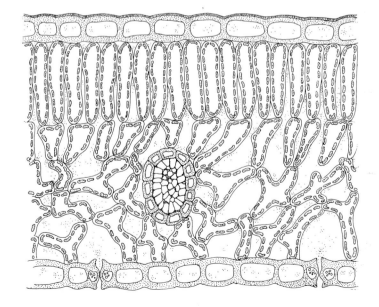

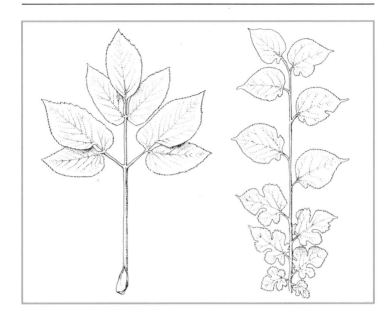

thesis. The characteristic bright green color of the chloroplasts is thus the green of the plant and is due to that residual luminous energy that is neither used nor absorbed by the chloroplasts when light travels through them.

The leaf's efficient capillary system of conduction is represented by the network of veins which run from the small base by which the leaf is connected to the branch, namely the *petiole* or *stalk*. As they branch out, the veins become ever thinner until they disappear among the cells of the chlorenchyma, to which they carry ground water, necessary for photosynthesis and for mineral salts, and from which they receive newly elaborated lymph. Both the chlorenchyma and the conducting bundles of the veins may contain cells of supporting tissue such as the aforementioned fibers (the tough, threadlike cells of which are dead) with a very thick, lignified wall, and *sclereids*, with walls similar to those of the fibers but short, irregular or star-shaped, and of a mineralized consistency.

The diversity of form and texture to be found in leaves does not apply to their internal structure, which alters only in the proportions and positions of the different tissues. Despite this, the variations in leaf shape are truly amazing. This is just as notable among the climbers as among the nonclimbers, and consequently there is no connection between the morphology of the leaves and the climbing habit. As Arthur Cronquist has observed, only a very tiny proportion of leaf shapes found in nature can be explained in evolutionary terms of ecological adaptation valid for all the angiosperms. Even so, the smaller, stiffer and tougher the leaf, the better it will adapt to dry climates (the extreme case being the leaves of the Cactaceae, transformed into spines); it is also true that in climates marked by an inclement season (cold winters or prolonged drought), the leaves tend to be of the deciduous type, dying and falling at the end of the favorable season, to be replaced by new leaves when these adverse

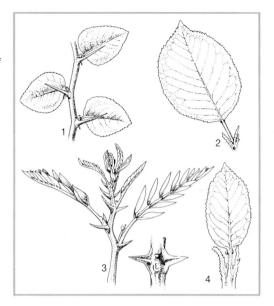

Opposite: leaf of podagraria in which a part of the sheath is visible at the base of the petiole, and leaf of mulberry with heteromorphous leaves. Right: leaves with normal stipules (2,4) and leaves transformed into thorns (1,3).

climatic conditions next occur.

The attachment point of leaf and stem is the *node*, and the length of stem between two successive attachments is the *internode*. The standard leaf type consists of three parts: *blade*, *petiole*, and *sheath*. The blade is the extended terminal part, full of photosynthetic tissue; its size and shape vary considerably from one species to another, sometimes even among individuals of the same population of a species, and even in the same individual. There is an official nomenclature to describe the principal types of blade shape. The petiole, which may be absent (sessile leaf), is the elongated axis which connects the base of the blade to the stem (or branch) of the plant; it may contain some photosynthetic tissue and its shape in cross-section may vary a good deal: cylindrical, angular, or flat. The sheath, when it exists, is a downward expansion of the petiole or of the blade itself, wrapping itself around part of the stem. The leaf may be accompanied, on either side of its point of attachment to the stem, by variously developed appendages called *stipules*, the importance of which is mainly taxonomic, associated with the recognition of genera and species. Other typical elements of the leaf are the pattern of the venation and the presence of hairs. The two principal classes of angiosperms, namely the dicotyledons (Magnoliopsida) and monocotyledons (Liliopsida) are also distinguished from each other by their prevalent type of venation: the former are net, the latter parallel. Hairs, more correctly described as *trichomes*, vary both in kind and in appearance.

Flowers

Rather than an organ, the flower is an apparatus, or a system of organs designed for sexual reproduction. It is a peculiar and exclusive attribute of

21

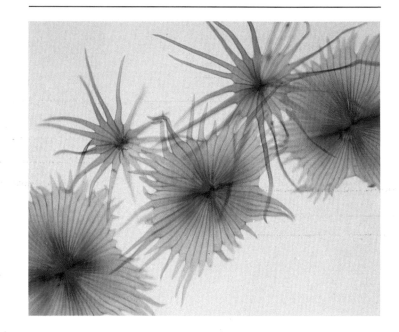

angiosperms, commonly known as flowering plants; it is not present in pines, ferns, and all other vegetable groups. In terms of evolution, however, the flower is not an invention of the angiosperms, which began to appear a mere 120 million or so years ago. Between 200 and 100 million years ago another group of plants made an appearance, achieved wide distribution, and then became extinct: these were the Bennettitales or Cycadeoideales, belonging to the Pteridospermophyta (a division that includes, for example, the present-day Cycadales), which produced primitive flowers, sometimes very large and showy, that were certainly visited by insects, and maybe by other animals.

The flower is made up of diverse organs of leafy origin, some assigned to producing the sexual elements, and hence fertile, others sterile, with the function of protecting the former and attracting those animals which, enticed by their color and scent, provide the invaluable service of pollination, in exchange for the nectar and pollen that provides their own nutrition. The flower may be supported by a stalk known as the *peduncle*, but it is the axis proper, or *receptacle*, which bears the different flower parts. The receptacle is expanded, in the shape of a club, a cone or a more or less flattened disk, convex or concave, or saclike so as to form a deep cavity. Attached to the receptacle are the sterile and fertile "leaves," arranged in concentric circles (*verticils* or *whorls*), or in spiral rows.

In the former type of flower, known as cyclic, the outermost whorl is made up of the *sepals* and is called the *calyx*. The sepals generally have a herbaceous consistency, are green like the leaves, and play an important protective role when the flower is in bud. Then comes the whorl of *petals*, known as the *corolla*:the petals are, as a rule, of delicate texture and brightly colored, their function being visually to attract pollinating insects. The combination of calyx

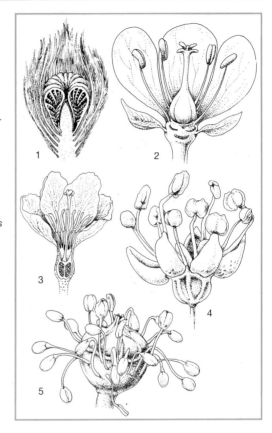

Right: 1. primitive "flower" of a fossil cycad; 2. complete flower with calyx and corolla (perianth); 3. monochlamyd flower without corolla (Hydrangea); 4. achlamyd flower without either calyx or corolla (Trochodendron); 5. flower with perigonium, without distinction between calyx and corolla. Opposite: microphotograph of scalelike, stellate hairs (trichomes) of prickly laurel.

and corolla, or sterile verticils, is known as the *perianth*. Sometimes there is a single whorl of sterile parts, made up of the calyx and corolla without any visible distinction between them: in this case the pieces, all equal in size, are called *tepals* and their whorl the *perigonium*. In other instances, one of the two whorls may be absent (either the calyx or corolla alone), and the flowers are described as *monochlamydeous*. When both whorls are missing, the flowers are said to be achlamydeous. The last two examples occur frequently in those plants which are not pollinated by insects but by the wind; indeed, in such circumstances the perianth would be an obstacle to air movement.

In spirocyclic flowers there are no whorls and the transition from sepals and petals to fertile organs occurs gradually, with parts of intermediate appearance. In this case, the parts are always abundant and variable in number (as, for example, in the water lily). In others, only some of the parts are arranged in a spiral, generally the fertile ones (*hemicyclic* flowers), the rest forming regular whorls with a precise number of parts (as, for example, the flowers of the genus *Schisandra*).

23

Right: the waterlily has a typically spirocyclic flower. Opposite: 1. longitudinal section of a flower with a superior ovary; 2. section of flower of Ribes cynosbati, *with inferior ovary; 3. section of flower of a rose, with numerous seminiferous ovaries concealed in the cavity (hypanthium) of the receptacle (calyx, corolla, and stamens not shown).*

Inside the corolla are the *stamens*, the male parts which collectively form the *androecium*. Each stamen is, as a rule, made up of a *filament*, either stemming from the receptacle or, sometimes, located on the inner part of the corolla, surmounted by an *anther*. The latter, when mature, opens to release the pollen produced inside.

The last, and innermost, whorl is formed by the *gynoecium*. This comprises one or more *pistils*, the female parts of the flower. The pistil is derived, like the other parts of the flower, from one or more specially transformed leaves, known as *carpels*. The carpel is a fertile leaf, thickened and virtually folded back on itself lengthwise, within which are produced *ovules*; these are, in effect, potential seeds. The tip of the carpel normally extends into a thin structure, the *style*, which terminates in an expanded *stigma*. Style and stigma jointly play a vital role in the process of pollination. The basal, enlarged part of the carpel that contains the ovules is called the *ovary*. Each pistil may either be formed of a single carpel (simple pistil) or, more frequently, of several carpels (compound pistil). In the wisteria, for example, the gynoecium consists of a simple pistil which, after fertilization, enlarges to become a pod. The flower of the clematis possesses a number of simple pistils, the styles of which lengthen, after fertilization, to take on the characteristic appearance of feathery tails; the ovary, therefore, is made up of numerous small, independent ovaries and is described as *apocarpous*. The majority of flowers, however, have a compound pistil, the edges of the carpels being fused to form a single, so-called *syncarpous* ovary. There are also intermediate cases, such as roses, where there are many small, independent (apocarpous) ovaries but in which the styles and stigmas are fused to form a column which projects just above the mouth of the receptacle.

The relative position of the androecium and gynoecium to their point of

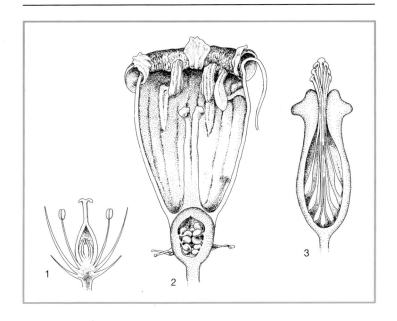

attachment to the receptacle is also an important consideration. The shape and development of the latter may give rise to three different situations. In the first instance the receptacle is hollow and its inner wall is united with that of the ovary contained therein; consequently the stamens, corolla, and calyx are placed high, in relation to the ovary, on the flat periphery of the receptacle. Here the ovary is *inferior* and the other parts are *epigynous* (as in the honeysuckle). The second case is similar, but there is a free space between the inner wall of the receptacle and the ovary, the upper part of which communicates with the outside; the entire cavity is called the *hypanthium*. Here the ovary is described as *semi-inferior*, while the other parts are *perigynous* (as in the rose). In the third situation the receptacle is flat or convex, bearing the ovary above the attachment point of the stamens and sterile verticils. Here the ovary is *superior*, with *hypogynous* stamens, corolla and calyx (as in the wisteria). In blackberries the top of the convex receptacle bears independent carpels (apocarpous ovary) which mature to produce a compound fruit.

Like the gynoecium, the parts of the other whorls may also, in some measure, be fused. When the sepals are fused, the calyx is described as *gamosepalous* or *synsepalous*; when the petals are fused, the corolla is *gamopetalous* or *sympetalous*. In the reverse instance, when the parts are separate and independent, the prefix *gamo-* and *syn-* is replaced by *dialy-*. Another very important aspect is symmetry. When, within each flower verticil, the parts are alike and regularly arranged, the flower is called *regular* or *actinomorphous*; if, however, some parts have different shapes and dimensions or are spaced in various ways, the flower is *irregular* or *zygomorphous*. Among the climbers, an example of a regular flower is the common passion flower (*Passiflora caerulea*), while the honeysuckle (*Lonicera caprifolium*) is irregular. As for the sterile verticils, both

Right: compound fruit of the raspberry, which mirrors the structure of an apocarpous ovary. Opposite, top to bottom: regular (actinomorphous) flower of Geranium sp. *and irregular (zygomorphous) flower of* Rhinanthus sp.

actinomorphous and zygomorphous flowers may be either of the dialy- or gamo- type. Zygomorphous flowers, in many instances, take on the likeness of "animals"; thus the papilionaceous corolla of the sweet pea (*Lathyrus odoratus*) resembles the wings of a butterfly, the spurred corolla of the flame nasturtium (*Tropaeolum speciosum*) looks like a small mouth, and the corollas of certain orchids are even capable of imitating the scents, colors, and markings of the females of their pollinating species, so that male pollinators are induced to make vain mating attempts.

The *nectaries* are areas of tissue capable of secreting nectar, the sugary liquid on which insects feed. As a rule the nectaries are scarcely visible, variable in appearance and occupying equally varied positions inside the flower. Most often they are found on a peripheral expansion of the receptacle known as the *disk*, but they may also be situated at the base of the sepals, petals, stamens, or carpels.

The distribution of sexes in flowers is also of great importance. Most frequently, the flower is as previously described, normally possessing functional stamens and pistils, and therefore said to be *hermaphroditic*, *bisexual*, or *monoclinous*. Often, however, flowers possess only one of the two types of sexual organ, behaving either as male or female. Such flowers are called *unisexual* or *diclinous*. Here, as a rule, there are two possibilities: either the plant produces flowers of both sexes, in which case it is a *monoecious* species (such as the pumpkin), or it produces flowers of one sex only and is a *dioecious* species (such as the kiwi). But there is a third possibility: the plant produces both unisexual and bisexual flowers in varying proportions, and the species is called *polygamous*.

Hermaphroditic flowers are very often observed to be *autoincompatible*, when

Right: gamopetalous regular corolla with patent tube and limb (Ipomaea).
Opposite: recurrent types of inflorescence; 1. raceme; 2. spike; 3. spadix; 4. capitulum; 5. umbel; 6, 9. compound raceme; 7. compound umbel; 8. panicle; 10. thyrse.

the pollen is incapable of germinating on the stigma of the same flower; functionally, therefore, they behave like unisexual flowers. Among monoecious and dioecious species pollination between different flowers is obviously the only possibility, but even in polygamous species this type of pollination is seen to occur. However, there are hermaphroditic flowers, to all intents and purposes, which practice self-pollination. Many of these, however, resort to self-pollination only in case of necessity (when there is little time at their disposal, before the onset of an inclement season, when pollinators are scarce, or when, as in violets, the flowers are repeatedly pulled off the plant). In the more "perverse" cases, however, self-pollination is normal practice. They include flowers that never open (as with violets) and self-pollinate already in bud, from which the fruit emerges directly.

Flowers are rarely solitary and are usually found in groups, on specialized branches, as this gives the plant better possibilities of reproduction. The combination of the flowers and the branches that bear them constitutes an *inflorescence*. These are divided into two major categories, *simple* and *compound*. The former have flowers borne on a single main axis (excluding, of course, the flower peduncle itself). Inflorescences of this type are the *raceme*, spike, spadix, corymb, umbel, *capitulum,* and *calathidium*. The flowers of the compound type of inflorescence are borne on secondary ramifications of the main axis (*partial inflorescences*) and include the *panicle*. The calathidium of the Asteraceae is particularly notable in that the main axis expands at the top into a receptacle (not to be confused with the flower receptacle already described) on which are inserted the flowers, all touching one another. In the subfamily Asteroideae, which comprises the daisies, the peripheral flowers (known as the *rays*) are completely different from the central flowers (of the *disk*). Whereas the

latter have a small, cup-shaped corolla, fringed by five (or, rarely, four) regular, outwardly folded teeth, the former have an extremely long and flared corolla, the *ligula*, often of a separate color, pointing outward like a ray. This inflorescence looks like a single flower, the center of which is actually formed of regular flowers and its margins of ligules, i.e. irregular flowers, which simulate petals. Another particular type of inflorescence is the *syconium*, typical of the *Ficus* species. The unisexual flowers, of both sexes, are contained in a kind of hollow, fleshy receptacle furnished with a small opening.

Pollen and pollination

Pollen is the dust, usually yellow in color, produced by the stamens and made up of millions of microscopic granules, the shape, size, and appearance of which are characteristic to the individual species. Each granule is responsible for the production of male sexual cells, the *gametes*. In order for the gametes to be conveyed to their female counterparts, contained in the ovules, the pollen *granule must come into contact with the stigma. This is the process known as pollination* and it represents the most critical moment in the life of a flower. Although the outcome of this process is strongly conditioned by chance, nevertheless evolution has effectively reduced the accidental element by fostering certain mechanisms that guarantee, at least statistically, the success of pollination. The oldest and most widespread of such mechanisms involve insects which, as carriers of pollen, travel from stamen to stigma and from flower to flower. The flower reciprocates by putting food substances, namely nectar, a source of carbohydrates, and pollen itself, a source of protein, at the disposal of those insects. The plant, in fact, is well equipped to produce a surplus of pollen so that a part of it can be used for fertilization.

There is a wide range of specialization between flowers and insects. In some flowers the nectar is stored at the end of a long, narrow corolline tube (for example, the Cape leadwort, *Plumbago auriculata*), visited by insects with a very long mouth apparatus, such as butterflies; some of these tropical flowers (such as the family Bignoniaceae) are pollinated by the tiny hummingbirds. Often the arrangement of the flower's internal organs is such as to compel the insect to become smeared with pollen in order to reach its food; when the insect visits another flower, it rubs against the stigma and deposits this pollen. The majority of flowers are pollinated by insects and among these so-called *entomophilous* flowers are the *zygomorphic* forms. But there are numerous species, in some cases entire families, which are *anemophilous*, i.e. pollinated by the wind. They are characterized by many inflorescences, sometimes soft and pendulous (catkins or *amenta*), of numerous small flowers, almost or wholly lacking a perianth, and so structured and inclined as to expose their anthers and stigmas to the slightest breath of wind. Anemophilous flowers obviously produce and expend a much greater quantity of pollen than entomophilous flowers because their type of pollination is that much more uncertain. The success rate is highest in dry, windy climates. There are also flowers, such as those of *Fallopia baldschuanica* of the Polygonaceae (see entry 24) which are both entomophilous and anemophilous, capable of being pollinated by both methods.

Once the pollen reaches the stigma, the sticky, sugary liquid that covers its surface attracts the pollen granules and induces them to germinate. Within a short time each granule then protrudes a *pollen tube*, which lengthens to grow through the style, digesting and feeding on its internal tissues. Continuing its growth, the tube reaches the ovary and, eventually, the ovule. Meanwhile, the *embryo sac* – a group of a few cells, two of which are the female gametes – has

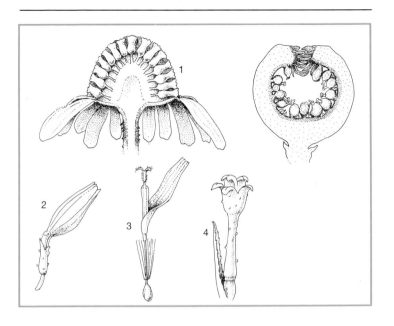

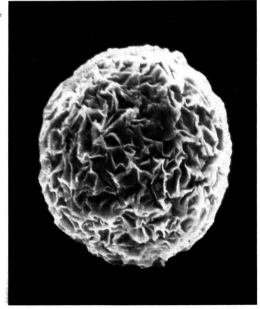

Above: 1. longitudinal section of capitulum of camomile with regular central florets and irregular peripheral florets. similar to "petals"; 2. sterile ligule with the function only of visual attraction; 3. fertile ligule functioning as female flower; 4. regular hermaphrodite flower.
Right: microphotograph of a pollen grain.

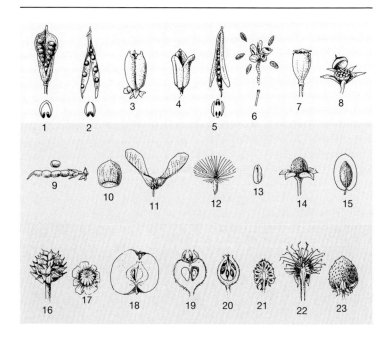

formed inside the ovule. When the pollen tube comes into contact with the embryo sac, *fertilization* proper takes place. The tube releases into the sac two male gametes which unite with their female counterparts to produce, respectively, the *zygote* (i.e. the first embryonic cell of the new seedling) and the initial cell of the *endosperm*, the nutritive tissue of the seed plant, the function of which is to feed the new plant during its early stages when it is incapable of carrying out photosynthesis. In some seeds this food tissue does not form, and in such cases initial nutrition is accomplished by the first leaves of the seedling itself, those already formed in its embryo, the *cotyledons*.

Fruit, seeds, and dispersal
After fertilization, everything changes. In some cases certain parts of the perianth, especially the calyx, may continue to grow, along with the maturing fruit. The ovary is enlarged and is transformed into a fruit, while the ovules inside become seeds, each of which contains a new seedling. The transformation into a fruit may follow two principal paths: in the first, the internal tissues become fleshy, juicy, and sugary, and the fruit takes on strong colors, most commonly red or black, the purpose of which is to attract birds, mammals, and even reptiles to feed on the contents, scattering the seeds, primarily through their feces; in the second, the tissues eventually dry up and do not turn fleshy. Here dispersal is extremely varied, using as agents either wind, water, animals, or even the fruit itself which uses a trigger mechanism to expel all its seeds simultaneously.

There exists a strict classification of fruits, based on the characteristics of the original ovary, namely the number of carpels, their rate of growth and whether they open along the margins or along the central vein. This scheme, however, is of little practical use for the present purpose, which is simply to describe the diverse types of fruit. For the sake of convenience, therefore, fruits may be divided into *dry* and *fleshy* kinds. The former are further subdivided into *dehiscent*, which, when mature, open and release their seeds, and *indehiscent*, which do not open, so that the fruit remains an integral part of the seed up to the point of germination. Indehiscent fruits contain, as a rule, one single seed and are sometimes furnished with one or more membranous growths which function as wings (aerial transport) or are covered with bristles or hooks (animal transport). Fleshy fruits are likewise of two types: the *drupe*, with an inner layer that enwraps the hard, woody seed, known as the kernel (such as the almond, walnut, cherry, and olive), or the *berry*, in which this inner layer does not become woody or is absent altogether (such as the pumpkin, blackcurrant, and so on).

As we have seen, certain seeds are dispersed together with the fruit (dry indehiscent fruits) or separately from it (drupe), while others fall straight to the ground. Both types are described collectively as *disseminules*. The disseminule may either lack entirely those "accessories" that facilitate its dispersal, or it may possess special structures that enable the wind or animals to carry it some distance: there are, for example, seeds provided with fleshy appendages that are much relished by ants which, in order to feed on them, carry them away and bury them.

The disseminules do not necessarily germinate as soon as they encounter favorable conditions of moisture and warmth; on the contrary, many of them enter a phase of *dormancy*. They contain special substances that prevent germination and are removed only after a given time, either by atmospheric

Opposite: 1–8. dehiscent fruits; 9–15. indehiscent fruits; 16–23. compound and false fruits. 1. follicle; 2. legume; 3. septifragal capsule; 4. loculicidal capsule; 5. silique; 6. explosive capsule; 7. poricidal capsule; 8. pyxidium; 9. lomentum; 10. nut; 11. samara; 12. achene; 13. caryopsis; 14. berry; 15. drupe; 16. multiple achene (Ranunculus); 17. schizocarp; 18. pome (Malus); 19. hip; 21. mora (collection of drupes); 22. multiple achene with grown styles (Geum); 23. multiple achene with fleshy receptacle (Fragaria); This page: 1. disseminule (fruit + seed) of Harpagophyton procumbens; 2. castor-oil seed whole and in cross-section, with embryo in endosperm; 3. haricot seed whole and in cross-section.

agents or by self-destruction. This allows the seeds to survive unfavorable periods, not only in respect to germination but also to successive phases in the life of the plantule. It is evident that if immediate germination is required, it is a matter of removing the layers of tissue, mostly situated in the outer shell or husk, which contain the inhibitory substance.

Germination and growth

Before cooking broad beans or lentils, it is necessary to soak them for a few hours in water to allow them to swell; if they are not too old, these seeds are perfectly capable of germinating and if soaked for too long will sprout rootlets which form a head in search of soil. Hydration of the seed is therefore the essential prerequisite for all the biochemical reactions that initiate germination. The seedling inside the seed is very simple, a small elongated stem, pointed at the tip. This tip is the departure point for the main root. In dicotyledons, on the other hand, the tip is bifurcate and each of the two forks is a cotyledon or embryo leaf. In the wisteria, sweet pea, vetch, and broad bean the two cotyledons are so large and thick that they occupy the whole volume of the seed, while the endosperm, the food storage tissue and companion to the embryo, is reduced to an extremely thin peripheral membrane. During the emergence of the seedling from the seed envelope, the large cotyledons, exposed to sunlight, may turn green for a while, contributing through photosynthesis to its nutrition; but they soon become yellow, wrinkled and dry. By contrast, in the Ranunculaceae (clematis, for example), the embryo is tiny, with barely discernible cotyledons, and the endosperm fills the rest of the seed. In this case, having consumed the stocks of the endosperm, the seedling emerges with two thin, green and expanded cotyledons which function, to all intents and purposes, as the plant's first pair of leaves. The seed of the morning glory and convolvulus contains, in almost identical proportions, endosperm and embryo. The latter has large, folded, bilobate cotyledons which, when they make contact with the light, swell and still remain green when the plant already has its fourth or fifth adult leaf. In monocotyledons (such as philodendron, black bryony, glory lily), the endosperm is generally well developed; the accompanying small embryo is provided with a single cotyledon which absorbs food directly from the endosperm during the hydration phase of the seed. The tip of the shoot then emerges and this soon turns green, producing the first adult leaf, while the cotyledon does not reach the light and degenerates after having exhausted the stocks of the endosperm.

Ecology, geographical distribution, and origin

The requisite factors of the environment that condition the life of a plant are respectively of a physicochemical and biological nature. The former are those that determine a direct response from the organism in terms of growth and vitality: the latter influence the behavior of the plant, especially as a result of living alongside and competing with other plants in the search for space and food. Other factors are the pressures exerted on the plant by animals, including humans.

Every plant depends for its survival primarily on the efficiency of its photosynthesis, and this also determines its reproductive efficiency. Good photosynthesis means good productivity. The four external factors that condition photosynthesis are temperature, water, light, and carbon dioxide. There are no problems regarding carbon dioxide (CO_2) because the amount present in the air, even at a height of 26,000 feet (8000 meters), is sufficient for a vegetable organism, such as a lichen, to live at that altitude. So the quantity of this gas available in areas given over to human habitation, particularly in towns and

The leaves and flowers of the wood sorrel (Oxalis acetosella) *open and close according to the duration and type of light rays that penetrate the underbrush by day.*

cities, far exceeds the needs of the vegetable world.

Nor are there problems with regard to light, at least in terms of the availability of solar radiation. But the duration of light, that is, the length of day in relation to night, may have an effect on vegetation. Thus there are *short-day* and *long-day* plants: the former, characteristic of intertropical zones, develop flower and fruit only if daytime illumination does not exceed twelve hours. This is why serious difficulties arose when tropical species such as the potato, tomato, rice, and corn were first imported into Europe. Conversely, long-day plants, typical of high latitudes, need much more than twelve (ideally, at least sixteen) hours of daytime illumination; for example, during the month of July, in the polar regions of the northern hemisphere, there is uninterrupted daylight, so that many plants of the tundra are perforce long-day species. In some cases it has been established that the opening and closing of the leaves are regulated by the chromatic quality of the light. For example, the leaflets of the sheep sorrel, a small plant that lives in the dim light of woodlands, stay wide open when, as has been verified, the blue component of sunlight is adequately represented.

Water is, of course, a fundamental requirement for any plant. In the heat of the midsummer months an average-sized pot plant left without water for a few days may wither, perhaps beyond recovery. In order to remain alive, a plant needs to transpire without interruption, absorbing water through the roots and dispersing it into the atmosphere through the stomata. Survival in dry surroundings thus depends on the plant's capacity to economize on water, to take advantage of all the available expedients to limit transpiration. Some of these expedients have already been discussed in the section devoted to leaves. As for water, the plant's adaptations are many and varied, so that at the extremes there are angiosperms that live in comparatively deep water – the

The glory lily (Gloriosa superba), *originally from the tropical zones of Asia and Africa.*

Najas species and *Posidonia oceanica* are found at a depth of up to 100 feet (30 meters) – and other plants that live in deserts and on arid mountain slopes.

The factor of temperature, finally, is crucial for cell metabolization. There is a lower limit beyond which any metabolic activity ceases. In the animal kingdom evolution has gradually overcome this problem with the development of warm-blooded organisms (birds and mammals) which maintain a constant temperature inside their body. Plants, on the other hand, have to contend with the outside temperature of the environment and when this falls below a certain point all their activities are curtailed. However, it is a strange fact that certain evergreen species manage to carry out photosynthesis even during the winter, on warm, bright days. Some conifers, like the Swiss pine, dwarf pine, and Norway spruce, photosynthesize even at below 32°F (0°C); but as a rule, it is more expensive for a plant to retain its leaves all year- round, with a little photosynthesis in winter, than to carry out the process only in summer and shed its leaves at the end of the season. For this reason, evergreen trees and shrubs are rare in temperate and cold climes.

Temperature also determines *phenological rhythms*, namely the annual recurrence of foliation, flowering and seed dispersal. A particularly long and cold winter can delay flowering, sometimes for up to a month. On the other hand, in species of the mountain lowlands, foliation and flowering are delayed in accordance with altitude. Naturally, the lower limit of temperature tolerated by a plant varies from one species to another, ranging, say, from the 77°F (25°C) acceptable to certain equatorial species to the -84F (-60C) of the graminaceous polar *Deschampsia antarctica*.

Excluding carbon dioxide, the availability of which is constant, temperature, water, and light become the three fundamental factors, responsible for the

36

variations in the planet's vegetational cover. To understand how they operate in determining the character of the vegetation, it is necessary to examine the problem in the context of each species which, in relation to the three aforementioned factors individually, exhibit an *optimum* of growth, below and above which there exist a lower and an upper limit of survival respectively. This is the result of natural selection which, over millions of years, has molded every species according to its own *habitat*. However, species seldom form pure populations, and as a rule mingle with one another in the search for food and space. Also, as well as water, plants need to find in the soil the mineral salts that are indispensable to their metabolism, and this is why they compete so readily with one another. Obviously, the closer each of these factors approaches to the optimum, the more aggressive and competitive it becomes. It follows that in nature, the more fully their ecological needs are met, the more successfully the plants live together. This is why, for example, a forest may appear internally organized and structured, with those plants that are less demanding in terms of light but more so in terms of humidity tending to form the lower layers (grasses and shrubs), whereas those needing more light and less humidity make up the forest canopy (trees). Plants also have varied needs related to the soil: these include type of reaction (acidity), circulation of air (dispersion), which depends in turn on soil compactness, and the thickness of the *humus*. In this sense, every type of soil has its own more or less specialized inhabitants.

The biological factors that influence plants are pollinators, disseminators, animal and vegetable parasites (fungi), and humans. The significance of the first two has already been described; parasites, on the other hand, are responsible for pathological states which, as they evolve, generally determine the vitality and resistance of the infected organism. Vitality and resistance are influenced by living conditions, implying that a species growing in a habitat that satisfies few of its natural needs will succumb more easily to the attacks of parasites. This is often verified in polluted artificial habitats, such as heavily industrialized cities, where plagues of certain parasites are facilitated by the difficult natural conditions of growth.

The very fact that plants had such diverse requirements for survival was therefore indispensable, from the evolutionary viewpoint, to their colonization of the planet; hence the origination of species typical of acid soils and cold-wet climates, rather than species of calcareous (basic) soils and warm-dry climates. It is interesting to note that even though such conditions are to be found in diverse zones around the world, it does not follow that the same species are always represented there. Indeed, in areas considerable distances apart, the resident species tend as a rule to be completely different. Every species occupies a determined part of the planet, namely its area of origin, and it can only be found in a different place if it has been introduced there. This, of course, applies exclusively to plants growing wild, not to cultivated plants.

Each species, therefore, has its own *geographical distribution area*. When the distribution of a species corresponds to a given territory, it is said to be *endemic* to that territory. It is worth noting that many species distributed by man, for economic reasons, outside their original territory, have escaped from cultivation, independently taking over new territories (such as the Japanese honeysuckle): their present-day distribution covers both the original and the new, distant, colonized areas. In some cases it is impossible to identify the origin of a species because there is nothing to indicate where it has come from. This is true of plants known today only in their cultivated form, such as the vine and the lentil, whose origins are lost in time. In other instances new "invaders" suddenly appear without having been intentionally introduced: these are plants whose seeds are accidentally transported in the course of commerce and other

exchanges of goods from country to country. The present-day distribution of species points to a broad variety of ranges and forms. Sometimes they consist of many zones, often far from one another (*discontinuous*); or confined to one or more mountain ranges; or comprising all or virtually all the land areas of the planet (*cosmopolitan*). And still others may be restricted to a few square yards of ground, even to a rock, a cliff, or a tiny island (*punctiform*).

In the study of plant distribution known as phytogeography, the assemblage of species populating a given territory is described as the *flora*. Each territory, therefore,has its own flora. But whereas some territories contain a flora that marginally overlaps a neighboring one, others resemble one another almost totally in configuration and size. The latter territories are as a rule clearly defined by physical and climatic factors such as orography, latitude, nature of soil, and so on. Such zones assume particular importance as potential centers of origin or of shelter for many plant genera and species. Among them are the mountain systems (Alps, Caucasus, Himalayas, Rockies, and ranges of Central Africa), islands (from Madagascar to the Galapagos, and others), the equatorial rainbelts of different continents, and so forth.

Climbers are represented virtually throughout the world.

Wild species, domestication, and cultivars

By beginning to cultivate several plant species of particular interest, our distant ancestors initiated a process of *domestication*. This implies the loss of certain characteristics of the original wild rootstock and the acquisition of new features which overall prove advantageous to man. In the course of this long and complex transformation, the basic factor is the choice of seed. Domestication does not have a single outcome but results in an assemblage of diverse forms

Opposite: originally from China, the wisteria (Wisteria sinensis) is now found everywhere.
Right: the Canary Island ivy 'Souvenir de Marengo' is an example of domestication.

that derive from different criteria of selection adopted in the area where those species are cultivated.

In the earliest stages of domestication there is the real possibility of spontaneous crosses between the cultivated plant and its original wild stock – a beneficial process that keeps the new variety genetically "fresh." As long as the two types flourish alongside each other, there is no disputing the origins of the cultivated varieties. But when these new varieties are quickly separated and distanced from the original wild populations, however, and when the latter come to be destroyed along with their surroundings, as has happened and is still happening in many parts of the world, all genetic exchanges are interrupted and the cultivated forms increasingly take on artificial characteristics, sooner or later exhausting their natural resources.

Sometimes cultivated species have degenerated, perhaps to the point of becoming extinct, even in recent centuries. Consequently modern agronomy, fortified by genetic engineering, endeavors to preserve the wild rootstocks that serve to rejuvenate and diversify traditional cultivated forms. One example of this is the tomato (*Lycopersicon esculentum*), into the genetic makeup of which attempts have been made to introduce genes of related wild species (*L. chmielewskii*, *L. glandulosum*, *L. cheesmarii*, and others), designed to obtain resistance to certain diseases, a shortening of the reproductive cycle, adaptation to saline soils, and other characteristics advantageous to their cultivation.

The domestication of climbing plants, as in all plants of economic interest, has very ancient origins. Moreover, they sometimes include species used for food. It could be argued that even the latter have a long history of domestication. But so, too, do very many climbers that possess purely decorative value, the wild ancestors of which are not always clearly defined. Among the modern climbers

The tomato (Lysopersicon esculentum) is the subject of continual experimentation in the genetic field, with a view to improving its productivity potential.

(as with many flowering plants) three principal situations may be distinguished: first, where the wild type still exists in nature and does not differ substantially from the cultivated type (such as *Campsis radicans*, *Bryonia dioica*, *Clematis [t40]tangutica*, *Akebia quinata*); second, where the wild type exists but its cultivated descendant is by now markedly different (such as *Cucumis sativus*, *Wisteria sinensis*); and third, where a wild type recognizably related to the cultivated type no longer exists (such as *Berberidopsis corallina*, *Passiflora edulis*).

The mechanism of domestication is not invariably the result of simply cultivating a wild species. Complex genetic phenomena often intervene, so that the cultivated form may derive from an initial hybridization of two related, but distinct, species.In other instances there are spontaneous mutations, namely variations that appear in nature and are extracted and isolated in cultivation. A consequence of domestication is the appearance, often on a large scale, of varieties and forms that are then selected for cultivation. The product is known as a *cultivar*, accentuating the fact that it had its origin in a cultivated form. Two cases may be distinguished here: first, where the cultivar appears spontaneously and in an unforeseen manner as a mutation or recombination within a cultivated population; and second, where mutants and recombinants are produced by selection as a result of techniques of applied genetics (treatment with colchicine, radiation, crosses, and so on).

Modern genetic engineering, increasingly capable of manipulating germ plasm and of directly intervening in the DNA of organisms, points the way toward genetic improvement of the product. It is to be hoped that it will find useful application in ecology, especially in programs designed to safeguard biological diversity, which is a real and urgent problem for the future of our planet.

Systematics and nomenclature

Not every plant has a vernacular or common name. A large number have never received a name in any language; perhaps even more are simply indicated by collective, generic names. For example, the names "convolvulus", "bindweed" and "morning glory" are applied to virtually all species of *Ipomoea*, *Calystegia*, and *Convolvulus*, just as "bignonia" is given to any species of *Tecoma*, *Tecomaria*, *Bignonia*, *Doxantha*, *Campsis*, *Clytostoma*, *Distictis*, and others. It is clear, therefore, that no matter how convenient, poetic, and suggestive the common name (where it exists) of a plant may be, on its own it is ambiguous and devoid of scientific value; all it has is a semantic content based on appearance, sensations, rituals, and uses, but seldom on observation of the vegetable organism itself. Also, the greatest inconvenience is that a plant may bear completely different names in various languages, making official accord impossible.

It was the eighteenth-century Swedish botanist Carolus Linnaeus who, with his *Systema Naturae*, finally established the principles of a hierarchic arrangement of living organisms which constitutes the foundation of modern taxonomic disciplines (botany and zoology) aimed at a faithful representation of biological reality. The basis of this arrangement is the *species*, well defined in the words of Arthur Cronquist as ". . . the smallest group of individuals, distinguished in a consistent and persistent manner, recognizable by ordinary means." Groups of species constitute *genera*, groups of genera *families*, groups of families *orders*, groups of orders *classes*, groups of classes *divisions*, and divisions finally making up a *kingdom*.

The names of all these categories are officially expressed in Latin, according to the International Code of Botanical Nomenclature.

Campsis x tagliabuana *is a noted interspecific hybrid obtained horticulturally by crossing the American* C. radicans *with the Sino-Japanese* C. grandiflora.

A "Chinese box" drawing that illustrates the taxonomic position of a climbing plant in the context of general botanical classification. Opposite: pruning a climber.

Conventionally, the name of every species is preceded by that of the genus to which it belongs, so that the organism can be expressed by a Latin binomial that gives its precise taxonomic identity. In the case of climbing plants there may be, in addition to the generic-specific binomial, other Latin and non-Latin names. These refer to the *infraspecific* categories, the possible variations within a species, such as the *subspecies* (subsp. or spp.), the *variety* (var.), the *form* (f.) and the *cultivar* (cv.), the last expressed by a name, not necessarily Latin, inside single quotation marks ('. . .'). In the case of hybrids of species, the specific name of the hybrid is preceded by the sign "x" (e.g. *Clematis x jackmanii*, *Lonicera x tellmanniana*), while crosses at infraspecific level, which mainly concern cultivars, are not indicated here because they are not within the scope of this book.

Finally, there is a reference to the names of authors and their abbreviations, which appear after the Latin description, as, for example, *Distictis buccinatoria* (DC) A. Gentry. The initials DC are an abbreviation of De Candolle, who originally described the species, which he named *Bignonia buccinatoria* DC. Subsequently Gentry claimed that this species should belong to a different genus and transferred it from *Bignonia* to *Distictis*: for this reason the name of the original author remains in parentheses, followed by the name of the reviser. The same procedure is followed in cases of changes in rank, from variety to species, from species to subspecies, and so on.

GROWING CLIMBERS

The cultivation of climbing plants requires neither more nor less effort than that needed for growing flowering plants in general. The only special need is for some kind of support suited to their particular method of growth. This will be discussed in due course. There is not general rule for cultivating climbers, since every species has its own requirements. These requirements are in no sense absolute, however, for each plant has a more or less broad range of adaptations to the essential factors of light, temperature, humidity, and soil. There are many highly demanding species, but they are outnumbered by the less demanding ones. There is obviously no point in trying to grow plants from climates that are very different from those of the places where they are to be cultivated without first creating artificially the conditions in which they will thrive. It is also important to bear in mind that climbers need space, because they have a luxuriant growth habit that often has to be tailored to the limited amount of room available to them.

Choice of species
When choosing a climbing plant to cover a wall, fence, or pergola, apart from its decorative quality, some thought should be given to "ecological" consider-

Right: ivy in flower. This species is well suited to shade and can be used in not too dry climates as an evergreen and honey plant. Below: the autumnal colors of the Virginia creeper (Parthenocissus quinquefolia).

ations, based on the geographical location and the natural potentialities of the place where it is to grow. It is better to use a climber that forms part of the spontaneous local flora than to go for a cultivar or exotic species. Why should it be, for example, that in Europe the Virginia creeper (*Parthenocissus quinquefolia*) is considered so much more aesthetically desirable than the common ivy (*Hedera helix*)? And why is it necessary to plant austere, funereal hedges of laurel (*Prunus laurocerasus*) when the native English hawthorn (*Crataegus monogyna*) is there to enliven spring with its bright flowers and winter, too, with its tiny scarlet fruits? Among climbers, too, the choice is often for evergreens, based apparently on the pretense or delusion that winter does not exist. Better to welcome the cold season in all its glory and learn to love and appreciate the bare outlines of plants that are dormant while they await the new cycle of growth.

When it comes to indoor plants, on the other hand, the choice of climber has to be exclusively aesthetic, depending on the available space, light, and humidity. The best climbing house plants are those that live naturally in tropical forests, under conditions of light and temperature that are easy to reproduce indoors. Atmospheric humidity, however, which is always high in the forest, may be rather less straightforward to reproduce.

The importance of climate: outdoor and indoor plants

Suitable climatic conditions are essential for the successful cultivation of climbers. There are species that are accustomed to every type of climate and to grow them outdoors depends on ensuring no marked differences between the climate of provenance and that of their adopted home. There are three main

*The creeping fig (*Ficus pumila*), a climber with clinging roots like the ivy, suitable for covering walls and fences.*

problem areas, relating respectively to temperature and humidity in winter, the duration of good weather, and the duration of daylight (photoperiod). Tolerance to minimum temperatures, but principally to the length of winter, is the factor that divides the climbers into three main groups: *hardy, half-hardy,* and *delicate* species. Hardy climbers tolerate low winter temperatures and periods, even quite prolonged, of frost: they include *Clematis montana, Fallopia baldschuanica* and *Schizophragma hydrangeoides.* Half-hardy species such as *Akebia quinata, Bougainvillea glabra, Plumbago auriculata, Trachelospermum jasminoides* and *Doxantha unguis-cati* can only withstand very short and occasional intervals of frost, and in colder climates have to be protected during winter in a greenhouse. Delicate species cannot tolerate the cold and need to spend the winter indoors or in a hothouse.

With regard to humidity, an important climatic consideration is the tension of atmospheric vapor. In hot or subdesert climates, the air becomes very dry during the summer months, with humidity values below 10 percent. In such conditions it is obviously unthinkable to try growing oceanic climbers such as the kiwi (*Actinidia* spp.), the Japanese honeysuckle (*Lonicera japonica*) or the Persian ivy (*Hedera colchica*) outdoors, even if winter temperature conditions are particularly good. It is a mistake to suppose that abundant watering can compensate for a dry atmosphere, because the plant's problem, in this case, is

Bougainvillea glabra, *the familiar and spectacular climber from South America, adapts well to zones with mild winters.*

its incapacity to transpire through the leaves, that is, to avoid water deficit. Plants such as *Smilax aspera*, *Clematis flammula*, *Eriocereus bonplandii*, *Tecomaria capensis* and *Delairea odorata*, on the other hand, come from climates with hot-dry periods and are therefore adaptable to zones where these conditions exist.

Many warm-climate climbers with a perennial habit and often woody-stemmed, may be grown even in temperate zones. Here, however, they behave as annuals and have to be resown every year. The duration of good weather (spring–fall in the northern hemisphere, fall–spring in the southern hemisphere) determines the climber's chances of concluding its cycle by producing seed. Very often (as in the mountains) this season is too short, so that it is necessary to anticipate seeding by one or two months either indoors or under glass, in a sunny, sheltered position, transplanting outdoors when there is no further risk of frost. The length of the growing season is a problem which obviously affects the perennial woody-stemmed species as well, particularly those that lack metabolic reserves for flowering and do so only following a fairly prolonged period of photosynthesis. One such example is the common passionflower (*Passiflora caerulea*), which in tropical and hot climes fruits abundantly, but further north often fails to flower and therefore brings no fruit to maturation.

The photoperiod may have a determining effect upon the flowering rhythms of certain climbing species. Tropical climbers are accustomed to a fairly constant period of daylight, although this never exceeds 12–13 hours. Conversely, in temperate latitudes, during the period around the summer solstice (northern hemisphere) or winter solstice (southern hemisphere), daylight lasts for 15–16 hours. It is hardly surprising, therefore, that in temperate climes many tropical species are "unsettled" during the growing period. Even so, with climbers, as with all domesticated plants, the photoperiod problem can generally be overcome. Many of the climbing Fabaceae and Bignoniaceae, for example, unlike their wild ancestral forms, have become indifferent to the duration of daylight. Thus it is not uncommon for a tropical species to produce cultivars that differ in their photoperiod requirements: those selected at high latitudes are indifferent, those selected in the tropics are short-day varieties. The lack of success in cultivating a tropical climber in a temperate climate can often be traced to the source, arising from the provenance of the cultivar and its natural light requirements.

For those who have no open ground or who prefer to grow climbers in pots or containers, a wide choiceis available, with a large number of species suited to this purpose. And the possibility of removing the container to a sheltered spot during the winter increases even further the number of growable species.

Indoor cultivation is all the easier if there are plenty of light, airy, humid places. The most usual problems are insufficient light and dry air. The former can generally be solved by using lucifugous (light-avoiding) species which in nature live in the shade, sometimes the deep shadow, of the forest environment. (Numerous climbing or clinging Araceae are ideal for this purpose.) The latter problem is more difficult to solve, as it is not easy to find many climbing species that are both lucifugous and xerophilous (adapted to a dry climate). It is therefore necessary to take steps to ensure that the leaves of a climber are surrounded by a constant, adequate level of atmospheric humidity, for example a moss-covered support. Classic indoor species belong to the genera *Monstera*, *Philodendron*, *Epipremnum*, *Cissus*, and others, which all adapt well to conditions in a house or apartment.

Preparation of the site

Choosing a site for planting a climber is important not only for aesthetic reasons but also to ensure successful results. When the plant is to be cultivated outdoors in the garden, some thought must be given not only to the general climate of the area but also to the microclimate, or the particular climate of the site itself. It is thanks to the microclimate that certain half-hardy or even delicate species can be grown in unfavorable climatic zones. Above all, the allocated space must be sufficient for the plant to expand, bearing in mind, for example, that the kiwi needs plenty of horizontal space, that the bougainvillea spreads mainly upward and the balloon vine (*Cardiospermum halicacabum*) normally manages to grow in a confined space. If need be, the plot should be cleared of any potentially undesirable climbers, even if it is only a question of a few dry remnants, so that the new plant can become properly established.

It is essential to give some prior consideration to the question of light, the likely formation of puddles, the space available for the roots, exposure to wind and salinity, and so on. Many houses have roofs that protrude, making it inadvisable to plant climbers at the base of the walls where the soil does not receive enough rainwater. The same problem applies to a covered porch which may similarly prevent rain falling directly onto the climber. If frequent work has to be carried out on walls or fences, it is best to use annual climbers such as morning glories or the Japanese hop, or species with annual aerial parts, like the common hop and the bryony. In this way there is no risk of destroying a perennial climber.

Having chosen the site, it is necessary to provide the support, should this not be naturally available. This may vary according to the type of climber selected and aesthetic considerations. In any case, planting out a climber is very simple provided it is done at the right time and in a manner suited to its requirements. Occasionally, prior to planting, some improvement of the soil may be

Right: kiwi (Actinidia chinensis) *in fruit. Opposite: a species of the Cucurbitaceae. Cultivation of climbers on balconies and patios involves more work than growing them outside in open ground.*

necessary.

To grow climbers on balconies and patios, all that is needed is plenty of good soil to fill the containers, bearing in mind that in comparison with the garden, container space is limited and thus liable to dry out. This type of cultivation consequently requires rather more effort and care; balconies, in particular, do not normally receive much rain because they are sheltered by similar balconies above or roofs that jut out. Top-storey balconies generally get more light and rainfall. However, even on lower-storey balconies it is sometimes possible to attach suitable plant containers to the outside of the railings, provided they are properly supported, in order to allow more rain to reach them. Rather than fixing the climber to the inside wall of the balcony, where light is poor and rain scarce, it is a good idea to fix a support, even one just made of wires, straight up from the railing, so that the climber can get better exposure.

Many climbers can be grown successfully in an enclosed space with little effort. A greenhouse, of course, is ideal for cultivating virtually all types of climbing plants but the function of this man-made environment is beyond the scope of this book. A *winter-garden* or *conservatory*, on the other hand, is a kind of compromise between a hothouse and a veranda, and a suitable annex to some houses and apartments. Above all, a conservatory provides excellent shelter for delicate climbers which need a lot of light even during the winter. Half-hardy climbers, accustomed to lower winter temperatures than those normally found in conservatories, pose more of a problem. These require an unheated spot but one that is well lit and exposed (an unheated veranda is ideal) which fulfills the function of a cool or temperate greenhouse. It provides shelter, for example, to many species from hot or subdesert climates which could not otherwise survive a winter in the open.

House plants must be kept well away from central heating radiators and positioned, if possible, near windows, but not in direct sunlight, because climbing indoor plants are as a rule lucifugous, originating in forests. The best results are obtained in large, bright rooms where the plants have plenty of space. They will also benefit from the fact that atmospheric humidity is that much higher in larger rooms.

Exposure

The cultivation of climbing plants in climates that are colder than their original habitat depends on the presence of particular microclimates, such as favorable conditions of light, temperature, and humidity. Such conditions exist naturally where the terrain is varied, as for example among hills, inside or outside a wood, or along the bank of a stream. Where the lie of the land is fairly uniform and featureles (as on a plain), however, it is houses, walls, streets, and the like that individually create a kind of microclimate. Even in cities small areas may be found where the average air temperature is markedly higher than that of the surroundings. This occurs in zones with poor air circulation where, in winter, domestic heating creates by emission a kind of "greenhouse effect," with abnormally high temperature levels. So what is defined as thermal pollution in cities may prove advantageous for the open-air cultivation of climbers that are not too hardy.

The most important aspect of the microclimate, however, is determined by the exposure. In low latitudes, where the inclination of the sun's rays is virtually the same in all directions, radiation brings about different effects according to exposure. In the northern hemisphere and, symmetrically, in the southern hemisphere, the incidence of solar rays is maximal on surfaces that respectively face south and north, minimal in the opposite directions and intermediate in exposures to east and west. By and large, in the northern hemisphere, a day of sunshine provides most heat to sites that face south and least to those that face north. In the southern hemisphere, conversely, the sequence is north–west–east–south. The reason why a west-facing site receives more heat daily than an east-facing site is that the latter receives direct exposure to the sun in the morning, only a few hours later than the night-time minimum, when the air and the ground are not yet warm, while in the former case the warmth of the afternoon sun is added to the already raised temperature of the air and the ground, providing even more heat.

Naturally, the relative humidity both of the air and the soil will also be influenced by the effects of exposure, tending to become lower in direct, prolonged sunlight. The less the air circulation, the hotter it will be. But the simple effects of exposure may be completely canceled out by other factors, such as wind. Favorable exposure may count for nothing if for local orographical reasons cold winds blow from that direction. Nor will a cool aspect have an effect if regularly subjected to masses of warm air.

Finally, the distribution and configuration of surfaces also have an influence on the specific features of the microclimate, in the sense that a simple flat surface may generate less heat than the angle between two walls or a recess that blocks air movement. Bearing in mind these simple facts, it is easy to understand why the orientation of walls, balconies, patios, and buildings in general plays a decisive role in the choice of a site and the opportunity to grow climbers outdoors.

Supports and containers

To some extent, the choice of support depends on the type of climber, and vice versa. If it is a question of covering a wall or smooth surface, the climber will have to be naturally furnished with clinging roots or adhesive pads, as for example *Hedera*, *Ficus pumila*, or *Parthenocissus tricuspidata*. Climbers with twining stems, suckers, and tendrils need to wrap themselves around supports that obviously must not be too thick. The most common solution is to use metal or plastic wire that is stretched and fixed as desired. This same kind of thin wire is used commercially to make up wide-mesh fencing, which enables the climber to grow more freely and uniformly. Narrow-mesh boundary fencing tends to crowd the climber so that the foliage overlaps, ending up by producing excessive growth at the top of the fence and loss of particularly unsightly if the idea is for the fence to be a visual screen. The use of wire or trellis on a wall is convenient for covering any type of flat surface with clinging or creeping species that otherwise would lack a suitable support. Trunks, posts, trellises, stakes, gates, low walls, heaps of stone, and cement borders all serve as potential supports. All climbers can wear away their supports, however, especially those whose clinging roots or similar organs find their way into gaps and crevices. Those with suckerlike pads cause less damage and will also adhere perfectly to the wire supports used for clinging types. These supports can also be used for constructing arbors, pergolas, gazebos, and the like.

The heart leaf (Philodendron scandens). For indoors, the best climbers are those that live naturally in tropical forests where conditions, humidity apart, can be artificially reproduced.

Right: a trunk can constitute an excellent support for climbers equipped with clinging roots or adhesive suckers. Opposite: Ficus pumila *and* Bryonia dioica *are two species that do not require special supports, unless allowed to spread.*

For pot plants the support can consist, for example, of one or more thin canes, slightly angled in a fan shape so as to offer the plant a broader area. Many indoor species (such as *Philodendron*) are often provided with a plastic pole, covered outside with moss or some absorbent material that remains moist for a good time after watering in order to increase the humidity level around the plant and stimulate the development of aerial roots from the nodes.

When choosing the type of container in which to cultivate indoor climbers, it is important to ensure, as far as possible, that conditions are fairly similar to those of the soil outside. Above all the container must allow for the free outflow of excess water through an opening in the bottom, which, if not present, has to be created. A 10-quart pot needs a hole 1[AC] in (3cm) across. Containers can be of earthenware, cement, wood or plastic, the first two giving the best results because of their porosity, which allows slow but constant evaporation through the walls, thus keeping the soil temperature sufficiently low. Wooden containers have the disadvantage of gradually releasing into the soil decaying lignin substances that may have an inhibiting effect on plant growth.

Impermeable plastic containers, which are relatively unaffected by outside variations of temperature, are widely used for seeding and transplanting but are not to be recommended as permanent pots. They are popular for indoor plants because of their lightness but this can be a disadvantage, for they do not provide a stable base. It is advisable, therefore, after buying an indoor climber, to transplant it from the plastic container (unless it is very large) into an earthenware pot. Heavy plastic receptacles can be purchased, containing a storage cavity which can be kept full of water, thereby avoiding the problem of having to water the plant continually from above. As a rule, the volume of the pot should be such as to allow the roots to spread, but contrary to general belief, a pot that is too large may be more harmful than one that is too small. Pots that are too large for the dimensions of the climber concerned are liable to cause root suffocation and consequent rotting from excess humidity: under such conditions parasites are likely to be more active. The space occupied by the roots should be proportional to the total transpiration surface of the plant, that is, to the quantity and quality of its foliage. In fact, in terms of space required, a plant with finely divided leaves has a much greater transpiration surface than one with entire leaves: the former will thus need a larger pot than the latter. Small or tiny pots are ideal for setting seed, and very small plastic or peat pots are sold for

Right: an indoor climber will grow best if it is sprayed at regular intervals so as to reproduce the rains of its tropical habitat. Opposite: a selection of tools for anyone wishing to grow climbing plants.

this purpose. The latter type are extremely convenient for seedlings because there is no problem of breaking the pot when transplanting.

The shape of the container is important, too, in determining the amount of soil relative to the capacity of the pot. The higher the ratio, the greater the evaporation and, hence, the more frequent the need for watering; conversely, a lower ratio implies more moisture retention and less frequent watering. The plant, for its part, contributes to the circulation of air by transpiration, the rate of which varies through the year and also from one species to another. It is evident that when the pot is small in relation to the aerial part of the plant, the soil dries out rapidly, largely as a result of transpiration, and that when the pot is big, moisture is retained for some time and its loss depends mainly on the shape of the container. Evaporation of the soil and transpiration of the plant combine to make up what is called *evapotranspiration*, which is manifested by the loss of water in the soil and conditioned by the relative air humidity. Xenomorphic climbers (those with the morpho-anatomical features of an arid environment) have a lower transpiration rate than others and do not therefore need large supplements of water, which they often store in their tissues (fatty plants); they can be kept in containers with comparatively high dispersal rates, for example low ones with a wide opening. The problem is just the reverse for climbers with a high transpiration rate, which require tall containers and/or a narrow opening. Broadly speaking, therefore, it is always better to use wide-mouthed containers so as to allow free air circulation. It is thus inadvisable to use amphoras or carboys and similar narrow-necked vessels which, if lacking additional openings, can lead to root suffocation.

For many indoor climbing plants, hydroponic cultivation is a possibility. This can be carried out in glass or transparent plastic containers and does not require too much care or special procedures, except periodic renewal of the food solution.

The substrate: soil, humus, and artificial media

Every species has its own soil requirements, as determined by four factors endemic to the substrate: *reaction*, *nutritive content*, *humus,* and *aeration*.

The *reaction* relates to the acidity of the medium. Every type of soil is more or less acid, the measure of acidity being the pH, with values ranging from 0 to 14. The intermediate value 7 indicates neutrality; below this acidity increases, above it the soil is basic or alkaline. As a rule, substrates that contain silica or compounds of silica exhibit acid reactions (from 4 to 6), while those full of carbonates (especially calcium and sodium) have an alkaline reaction (up to 11). The proportions of these components varies continuously from one soil to another, so that every level of acidity or alkalinity may be encountered. For example, soils derived from loam, the sedimentary rock formed from clay and limestone, have a low pH when the former predominates, and vice versa. Some substrates, such as peat, that contain neither silica nor limestone, display an acid reaction by reason of substances that form as a product of the biological decomposition of cellulose and lignin. The same is true of the humus of conifer woods, where the strong accumulation of lignin determines marked acid-ification of the upper layers of the soil. Conversely, the humus produced by many broad-leaved trees ranges from acid to alkaline. From the practical viewpoint, when a soil is too acid, its reaction may be corrected by the addition of limestone; and when it is too alkaline, it can be given acid peat or silica powder. Among the climbers, there are a few rare cases of markedly acid-loving

Right, below and opposite: examples of experimental hydroculture. This is a technique that can be used for growing many indoor climbers.

species, e.g. *Nepenthes*, which have to be cultivated in peat, although the other extreme tends to be more common. Generally, however, climbing species are adaptable to a broad pH range, and the acidity in the soil has relatively little impact. This is hardly surprising, as selective cultivation has certainly favored the more adaptable types.

The *nutritive content* of the soil denotes nutrients that comprise the nitrogen compounds and phosphorus (carbon derives from photosynthesis) indispensable to the plant for the production of proteins and nucleic acids; it also comprises potassium, magnesium, iron, manganese, lithium, and other rarer elements, involved mainly in the functioning of enzymes. Better nutrition generally means better development but, through natural selection, plants have evolved various strategies in this regard. Species from poor soils generally lose their vigor if grown in rich soils, and vice versa. There are some species, such as the passionflowers and the flame nasturtium (*Tropaeolum speciosum*), which in rich soil, namely one with high nutritional content, expend all their energy in strengthening their photosynthetic apparatus, their stems and leaves, at the expense of flowers. These plants come into flower when their nutritive stocks begin to dwindle. So this is an example of excessive feeding having undesirable results. However, feeding is necessary when the soil is visibly poor, especially for pot plants which, by reason of limited space, are easily weakened as a result of watering. In such cases the best procedure is a complete change or remixture of soil.

On any soil surface, the dead vegetable (or animal) material that continues to accumulate forms a layer of organic detritus known as *litter*; this layer, starting

Right: the fertile soil of orchards is ideal for growing climbers such as the sweet pea. Opposite: the wisteria, like most plants, enriches the soil with nitrates.

from the bottom, is subjected to biological decomposition (humification) through the activities of small animals, fungi, and bacteria. The products of decomposition are rather complex organic molecules (fulvic acids and humic acids) that are soluble in water and are "captured" in a more or less stable manner by the clay in the underlying soil layers. From the *clay-humic complexes*, together with other mixtures of decayed products deriving from organic matter, are formed the *humins*; and all this constitutes the *humus*. There are different types of humus, according to the water content, the stability of the clay-humic complexes, the presence of soluble (thus mobile) acids, or the effect of calcium, which renders it insoluble (thus immobile). The humus texture is reflected, of course, in different methods of cultivation. A peat humus, for example, is a determining feature suited to the growing of *Nepenthes* species, whereas a broad-leaved humus is better adapted for use as ordinary house plant soil.

As a rule the soil sold by florists and supermarkets is not humus, but more or less decayed litter, without a clay component and enriched artificially with organic salts and minerals. Such soil on its own is useless and should be mixed with natural earth, its only function being to restore and improve poor soil that has been reduced to its basic minerals, enabling it to resume some biological activity.

Finally, *aeration* is essential for the roots which are engaged in absorbing and diffusing liquids by osmosis, a task that requires a high measure of respiratory activity. Air circulates freely in the soil through spaces known as pores, and the amount of space is conditioned in turn by *particle size*. When the particles are

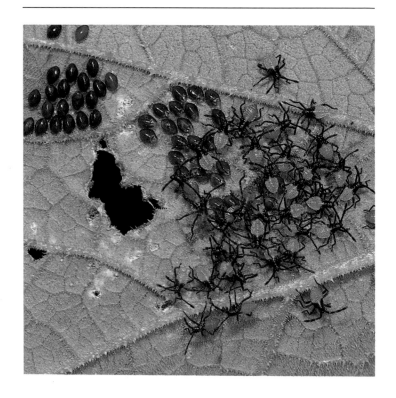

large, the pores are more fully occupied by air, circulation is very efficient, and the soil texture is loose, light, and well drained (sandy). When the particles are tiny, however, the pores have less room for air, circulation is much slower, and the soil is compact and heavy, with virtually no drainage (lime and clay).

A certain number of species are adapted to living in conditions at either of these extremes, but the majority can settle for somewhere in between. However, when cultivating climbers it is important to know the texture of the soil at your disposal because both light and heavy soils are to be found everywhere and some may be unsuitable. A heavy soil may need to be improved with a mixture of humus and sand, while a sandy soil can be given more cohesion and water-retaining capacity by adding clay and humus. In agriculture standard mixtures known as *composts* are used. These are available commercially and are used especially for sowing seed and for propagation. To improve moisture distribution and aeration inside the pot, it is advisable, before introducing the soil, to place a thin layer of shards on the bottom, without covering the hole or drainage slits. The shards help to keep the soil moist through capillary action, gradually introducing water from outside the pot and ensuring better air circulation inside, without the risk of sudden drying out.

There are many hydroponics techniques, some suitable for indoors, whereby the solid medium represented by soil is replaced by the liquid medium of water. Hydroponics is simply the growing of plants in water with the addition of special

Right: a species of locust (family Cicadidae) on the leaves of Philadelphus coronarius. Opposite: a leaf attacked by young bugs of the family Lygaeidae.

pellets (ion-exchanging resins) which furnish the food solution with the necessary minerals and have to be renewed as they are used up. This soilless culture can be performed with any type of container, preferably of dark glass to enable the roots to develop more evenly; the root system must be thoroughly washed and cleaned of all residues of soil and other material prior to being soaked in the solution. Another method based on hydroponics is to fill a solid-base container with shards, set the climber in position and pour in a sufficient amount of food solution (no more than halfway up), topping it up every now and then.

Diseases

Like all plants, climbers are subject to diseases, sometimes difficult to diagnose, which slow their development, weaken them, prevent them from producing flowers and fruit, and often kill them. There are many reasons why a plant may become sick and for the most part not solely from the effect of a particular pathogenic agent but of a generalized syndrome. The most widespread symptom of a plant's ill health is *chlorosis*, the yellowing of its green parts, which as an initial reaction reduces or suspends the synthesis of chlorophyll (green), while maintaining the caretenoid pigments (yellow). The original causes are, as a rule, of a dual nature; physicochemical imbalances of the growing environment, which are manifested in the plant as physiological deficiencies,

and parasites. If the disease is uniquely physiopathic, the remedy, once the cause has been identified, may be very simple: the most frequent example occurs in house plants, which often tend to turn yellow and dry out due to the excessive dryness of the air. To create a sufficiently humid atmosphere in such situations, it is necessary to spray the leaves frequently. The yellowing of the foliage may also be caused by imbalances of the soil: the commonest cause here is lack of iron, an indispensable element for the functioning of the enzymes associated with the synthesis of chlorophyll. In some cases the iron may effectively be absent but more often the plant fails to absorb the iron present in the substrate because the latter is too calcareous (limestone chlorosis). This problem can easily be avoided by administering *sequestrenes*, substances that are capable of releasing the iron gradually in response to the needs of the plant. In sensitive species, chlorosis can also be due to cold; but as conditions return to normal, regular synthesis of chlorophyll is resumed.

Diseases may equally be caused by excesses: too much water around the roots can bring about suffocation, with the possibility of *necrosis* and rotting of the tissues, while the provision of too many nutrients by overfeeding may inhibit growth, provoking chlorosis and desiccation. Deficiencies can also originate in defective or excessive lighting: the former is more frequent and causes the plant to become spindly, with abnormal lengthening of the internodes of the stem, which looks weak and whitish compared with the leaves (*etiolation*), so that neither chlorophyll not caretenoids are synthesized. Too much light produces chlorosis, spotting, and desiccation. Both situations can be remedied: it is possible nowadays to buy sun lamps that stimulate photosynthesis, thus overcoming the problem of insufficient illumination. The remedy for excessive lighting is to provide adequate shading or to avoid exposing the climber to the direct rays of the sun.

Serious trouble begins when the health of the plant is threatened by pathogenic agents, namely parasites that may comprise viruses, bacteria, fungi, nematodes, spiders, and insects, all of them organisms that live on the cells and tissues of the host. Although a distinction is properly made between diseases caused by the first three groups and those caused by animals, this is obviously a matter of form rather than substance. Whereas many pathogens may attack the plant regardless of its state of health, they tend to be most successful when the plant is already to some extent debilitated; one parasite often prepares the way for another, thus contributing to the eventual demise of the host. In this context it is worth mentioning that, through the effect of normal genetic variability, each individual plant born from seed has its own measure of vigor and capacity to resist pathogenic agents; as a rule, therefore, one package of seeds will produce some plants that are sturdy and aggressive along with others that are weaker and more susceptible to attack by parasites. Naturally, horticultural selection always opts for those with greater resistance, but since parasites themselves "learn" to be selective, occasionally developing strains capable of attacking new cultivars, the problem can never be said to be wholly resolved.

Certain viral and bacterial diseases cause malformations or monstrosities (such as tumors and fasciations), others blackening and decay or abnormal proliferation of organs and tissues; however, these forms of disease are not all that frequent. Many more are caused by spiders, insects, and fungi. Particularly troublesome to climbers, and especially the indoor species, are the red spider mite, whitefly, aphids, and scale insects. The main harm done by these pests is that they extract lymph from the plant by perforating with their mouthparts the walls of the sieve tubes; as a result, the plant is enfeebled, fails to flower, and

Right: leaf with the symptoms of a fungus disease. Opposite: adult bug of the Lygaeidae. with typical leaf-gnawing effects.

often suffers a slow death.

The infested plant generally reacts to the parasite attack by emitting a sugary liquid, honeydew, on which the parasite feeds; the honeydew, especially in wet weather or after normal watering of the plant, may then induce the development of a blackish deposit known as sooty mold, caused by saprophytic insects that feed on dead or decayed matter, which lowers the rhythm of photosynthesis, reduces the plant's vitality and spoils its appearance.

Because these parasites often show resistance to preparations designed to combat them, they are not easily destroyed; and although toxic chemicals are a possibility outdoors, they cannot safely be used indoors. Consequently, when a climbing house plant shows signs of being badly attacked, it is often more convenient to throw it out than to attempt to eliminate the infestation. If chemical and biological remedies are used outdoors, scrupulous care must be taken to follow the instructions for use, keeping children and animals well away from the place where the plants are being treated.

The larvae and even adult forms of many beetles, butterflies, and moths may all

Right: the defoliating effects of an attack by phytophages on Medicago sativa. *Opposite:* Popolia japonica *on rose buds; this is a beetle from the far East that has spread to most parts of the world.*

do harm, for they feed on the leaf tissues of the plant, causing erosions and perforations which, at worst, bring about complete defoliation. As a rule, however, the damage done by these phytophages is less serious than that of other parasites. Certain small wasps can also bore tunnels in the leaf, feeding on the mesophyll; apart from unsightly appearance, there are no other grave consequences.

There are many fungal, bacterial, and viral diseases that provoke a wide variety of different symptoms. These diseases, too, are difficult to cure, ranging as they do from simple blemishes to deformation, withering, and death of the plant. Fungal mycoses, caused by organisms belonging to the Oomycetes, Zygomycetes, and Ascomycetes, often produce whitish or bluish coatings, with the appearance of mold, on the leaves and stems. The vegetative part of these organisms, the mycelium, lives and develops inside the tissues of the host; and the coating is produced by the organs of dissemination (*cones* and *spores*) that jut out from its fertile ramifications. Other species of fungus are responsible for spots, streaks, deformation, or desiccation; yet others cause mold and rot. They can all be tackled with chemical products specific to particular combinations of physical parameters (temperature and humidity).

Chemical products must always be used with the utmost care, according to instructions as to method and frequency. Parasites cannot be eliminated at any given moment but only during particular phases of their life cycle the spores are about to germinate and infect the host. Certain mycoses and bacteria can be fought by biological means but such applications are for the most part still experimental. As for viruses, which are responsible in general for malformations, fasciations, proliferations, depigmentations, and other problems, the ideal solution is to remove the affected parts, providing this will not seriously damage the plant.

Propagation

The methods used for propagating a climbing plant are the same as those employed in agriculture. There is an advantage, however, in that climbers are generally competitive plants, capable of spreading freely, throwing out stems and branches in all directions. Their vegetative strength, however, is dependent upon a high measure of meristematic potential, the capacity of their vegetative parts to reproduce new tissues and new organs. Because of this characteristic, climbers are among the easiest plants to propagate by the traditional vegetative methods: *cuttings*, *division*, *layering*, and *grafting*. The main advantages of vegetative or *agamic* multiplication are its simplicity and the fact that it preserves unaltered the characteristics of the climber from one generation to the next. It is a fact of genetics that all asexual reproduction results in the formation of individuals identical to one another and to the original parents.

Propagation by cuttings consists in removing a branch, leaf, or root, placing it in water or directly into soil, and thus obtaining a new plant. The soil must be loose, to guarantee good aeration, but at the same time very moist, to induce the

formation of new organs. The three types of stem cutting are softwood or herbaceous, semiripe, and hardwood. Softwood cuttings are taken from the young shoots of perennial, herbaceous, or suffruticous (with a woody base) climbers, cutting the shoot beneath a node (in *Clematis* midway along the internode). It is best to choose shoots that are not too long, up to about 4 inches (10 cm) and, above all, not flowering, because the metabolic effort of flowering would prevent the shoot from concentrating its energies on throwing out roots and producing leaves. As there is no particularly favorable period for taking softwood cuttings of house plants, it can be done at any time of year; but the best period for outdoor climbers is June–July.

Semiripe cuttings are taken from partially lignified shoots not less than 4–6 inches (10–15 cm) long from shrub or tree climbers. Outdoors this can be done in summer (June–September), making an oblique cut just beneath a node, removing all the leaves from the branch below and taking off the apical shoot to make it easier for the roots to form and spread. Semiripe cuttings should be buried one-third to two-thirds of their length in a substrate with the same features as for softwood cuttings. However, they take much longer to root, depending on the species and prevailing conditions. It is important to remember this and to make sure that the soil in the small pots used for rooting

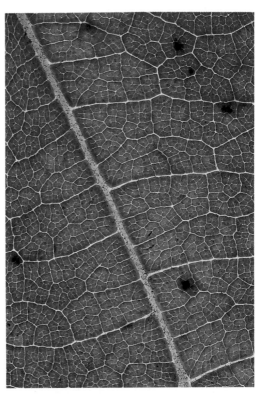

Right: the traces of a parasite on the underside of a leaf. Opposite: aphids perforating the sieve-tubes of a plant to suck out the lymph.

does not become impoverished too soon, losing its essential nutritive substances.

Propagation by means of hardwood cuttings is seldom used for climbers; it is much easier to remove the shoots. However, these are well-lignified branches, 6–16 inches (15–40 cm) long, taken during the period of winter dormancy, just beneath a node and with the removal of the apical shoot if the latter is not completely woody. The cuttings are normally buried directly in the soil, outdoors, to about one-third to two-thirds of their length; rooting will take between six months and a year. Because of this much longer waiting period, such cuttings aregenerally more successful than the others described.

Certain outdoor climbers can be propagated by means of root cuttings, taking roots ¼–¾ inches (0.5–1.5 cm) thick and 2–6 inches (5–15 cm) long. This should

Right: this type of support for a philodendron retains humidity for a long time, inducing the plant to throw out aerial roots which provide an easy means of vegetative propagation.
Opposite: example of grafting.

be done during the dormant season (fall-winter), cutting the root horizontally and also the tip of the root obliquely. The stump is then set vertically, until totally covered, in loose, rich soil, and rooting takes place in early spring; if the cutting is in a pot, later to be set outside, do not transplant until the following fall.

Finally, there are leaf cuttings, obtainable from fleshy-leaved climbers such as *Delairea odorata*, *Basella rubra*, and *Anredera cordifolia*. Leaves are removed, complete with stalk, and buried stalk upward in light, sandy, moist soil, with the leaf blade protruding. This operation is done in surroundings with a temperature of 61°–65°F (16°–18°C); after a time that varies according to species, small shoots appear at the base of the leaf. Even with these suitable climbers, however, other methods of propagation are to be preferred as the outcome of the leaf-cutting technique is likely to be rather uncertain.

Another important form of propagation is by division, which is practiced on climbers that grow in clumps, with numerous stems that are joined at the base or produce suckers, and on all species furnished with rhizomes, underground stolons and tuberous roots. In the dormant period (fall-winter) the whole plant is removed from the ground and the clump divided with clean cuts into two or more pieces that are then replanted separately. This technique has the advantage of rejuvenating old stock, and the new clumps quickly start to regrow.

Layering consists of inducing segments of stems or branches to produce live roots that are then detached to develop independently. The method exploits the tendency of all plants, even those incapable of yielding cuttings, to root their aerial parts when these bend downward to touch the ground. This is a fairly common phenomenon in nature, particularly among climbers and drooping

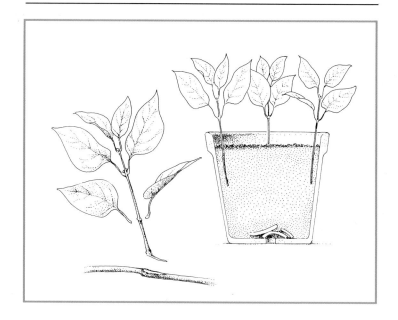

species; as a propagation technique it is notably successful.

In cultivation, the layer is obtained by taking a flexible, reasonably long, healthy, and vigorous one- or two-year-old branch and bending it downward until it touches the soil. An incision is made to stimulate production of new tissue; the cut part of the branch is then buried and fixed with an iron hoop or other support to keep it in position. Rooting is very slow (perhaps one to three years) but is guaranteed. The best period for layering is fall, when the plant enters its dormant phase.

Air-layering, a technique practiced on plants with stems or branches that do not easily bend, is rarely used for climbers, except when there is no alternative. In spring or fall, make an oblique cut in a one- or two-year-old branch, 6–8 inches(15–45 cm) from the tip, covering the wound with sphagnum moss or inert material to prevent scarring. About 4 inches (10 cm) above and below the incision, bind the ends firmly in a sleeve of polythene or transparent waterproof material previously filled with a mixture of peat and sand or or compost. When the roots appear through the covering, cut away the branch and plant it in a pot prior to placing it permanently outside.

Climbers that throw out stolons (shoots from the base of the plant), are often propagated in this way. The stolons sprouting from the nodes are set either in the ground or in a pot, held by metal or plastic tacks; when growth appears, the stolons are cut off and the new seedlings planted separately.

Grafting, widely used in fruit cultivation, is something of an unknown quantity where climbers are concerned, employed as a last resort if all other methods are impracticable. In any event, from the biological point of view, it is not a genuine

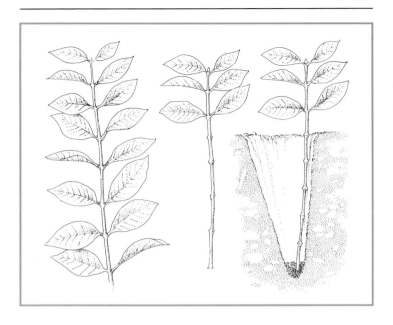

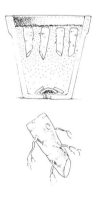

Above: woody cuttings. Above: root cutting. Right: semiripe cutting.

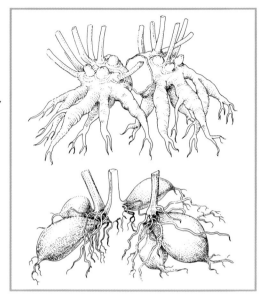

Right, top to bottom: propagation by clump division in a rhizomatous plant and one with tuberous roots. Opposite, top to bottom: propagation by root suckers, tip layering of a blackberry and (below) an example of grafting.

method of propagation and needs no further discussion here.

The most natural means of multiplication, of course, is by seed, the outcome of sexual or gametic reproduction; and for climbers with an annual cycle it is the only possible method. Sexual reproduction, unlike agamic reproduction, produces variable descendants, so that in every generation individuals with new combinations of characteristics may appear, even though the variability may seem to be very slight or nonexistent. In practical terms it has both advantages and disadvantages, especially in the flower-growing field. The principal advantage is to be able to select individuals that exhibit characteristics deemed to be useful, for example sturdiness, flower color, rapidity of the plant cycle, or resistance to certain diseases. Numerous individuals can be obtained from a single seeding operation, whereas a cutting or a layer produces only one. In the case of half-hardy species, too, it is possible to isolate seeds from a given generation so as to favor those plants that show greatest resistance to cold.

Among the disadvantages are the time needed for growth, undoubtedly longer than with cuttings, and above all the impossibility of preserving certain characteristics in the descendants when the parent is a hybrid. A high proportion of cultivars of many climbers are in fact the product of crosses between species and varieties, reproduced solely by vegetative techniques. The combination of features present in a hybrid is not preserved during the sexual reproduction of the latter, so it is not possible to resort to seeding. Furthermore, true hybrids (crosses among species) are sterile and cannot produce seeds, or only in very small quantities and with little vitality.

Seeds are normally set in boxes or small pots, preferably of peat, at an optimal

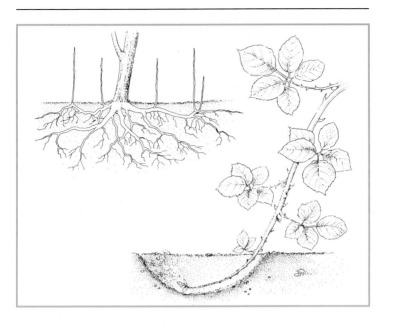

73

Left: Clematis jackmanii, *a climber that is pruned in February. Opposite, left to right: pruning of* Clematis montana *and* C. tangutica. *In the former, which flowers on the wood of two years: branches must be removed after flowering, while in the latter, which flowers on the current year's wood, pruning should be done at the base in spring, when put outside. A year later the branches near the base are pruned, leaving a few shoots to originate new buds.*

temperature of 61°–68°F (16°–20°C), and covered with a thin layer of soil. Lack of success is often due to the seeds being set too deep. The soil, which for preference should be a mixture of peat, sand and compost, is lightly watered after sowing, ideally from the bottom, by capillary action. Annual species with a long cycle are best begun in February–March under glass (or plastic) in a bright, sheltered spot.

If not planted immediately, the seeds should be kept under a layer of dry sand in a cool, dry, airy place. As a rule it is inadvisable to use seeds more than a year old because as time passes they tend to lose their capacity for germination. The seeds of some delicate indoor climbers have an extremely short germination period of not more than a week and should be sown immediately; in other cases (*Cardiospermum halicacabum*), the seed may remain viable for more than ten years.

Pruning

Pruning, which is designed to encourage the production of shoots, is not necessary for many climbers but essential for others. Those that do not need such attention, except for the reason of containing their uncontrolled growth, include freely growing outdoor species such as ivy, Virginia creeper, and Japanese honeysuckle. Obviously, delicate indoor climbers of the *Cissus* and *Philodendron* type are never pruned. But the climbers growing on pergolas and trellises can do with pruning either before or after flowering. There are, in fact, species that flower either on the branches of the previous year or of the current year. The former have to be pruned at the end of winter, before flower buds appear, eliminating all dry branches and twigs; the latter are generally pruned in the fall, after flowering, to encourage the formation of new flowering branches

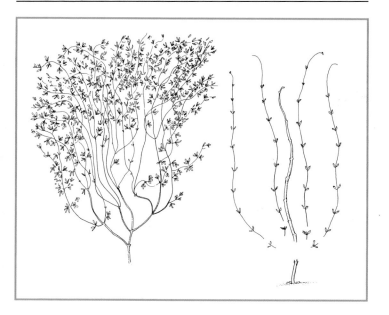

the following spring. Numerous climbers are grown for their foliage (*Vitis* spp., *Cocculus* spp., *Menispermum* spp., and others): if they are evergreens, pruning should be done in early spring, but the opportune time for deciduous species is in winter. Certain half-hardy climbers that would otherwise be damaged by cold or die off in winter require drastic pruning, before the first frosts arrive, down to ground level, removing all aerial plants of the plant and at the same time protecting the base with plenty of foliage, straw, wood chips, pieces of cork, or polystyrene.

1 LYGODIUM FLEXUOSUM (L.) Sw.

Order Filicales.
Family Schizaeaceae.
Origin Southeast Asia.

Description Herbaceous perennial plant with pinnate leaves of indeterminate growth, made up of primary leaflets (pinnae) in turn divided into secondary leaflets (pinnules); the latter are further divided into segments. The upper leaves are often fertile and differ from the others in appearance, being narrower and with the last segments characteristically fringed.
Dispersion of spores Occurs in summer.
Cultivation This tropical climbing fern is suited to conservatories and temperate greenhouses. Rich, cool, loose soil, in shady but bright position. Remove dead leaves. Because of its delicate foliage, it should be allowed to twine around other plants so as to avoid leaving unsightly stakes visible.
Propagation By division in spring, by spores in summer.
Use Markedly vertical growth, up to 65 feet (20 m); also suitable indoors.

2 PIPER NIGRUM L.

Common name Black pepper.
Order Piperales.
Family Piperaceae.
Origin Eastern India and Malaysia.

Description Vigorous shrub, the lower part woody; twining stems, up to 23 feet (7 m) long, with clinging roots at the nodes. Leaves persistent, petiolate, alternate, coriaceous, pointed at tip, cordate at base, with prominent veins. Flowers unisexual (dioecious plant) in dense greenish spikes, axillary, without perianth. Fruit (drupe) spherical, initially green, then pinkish, black when mature.
Flowering period Summer.
Cultivation Tropical plant grown outdoors where temperature does not drop below 65°F (18°C), otherwise in hothouse with high air humidity, sprinkling foliage frequently. Cool, well-drained soil, in shady position. Partial pruning encourages formation of new shoots. Needs support when young.
Propagation Normally by cuttings, alternatively by layering or air-layering.
Use Indoors only if surroundings are sufficiently cool. Quickly forms carpets. The partially mature fruit is dried, constituting black pepper.

3   ARISTOLOCHIA ELEGANS Mast.

Common name Calico flower.
Order Aristolochiales.
Family Aristolochiaceae.
Origin Brazil.

Description Fast-growing herbaceous perennial plant with sturdy, branching stems. Long-stalked, ovate-cordate, persistent leaves. Large, showy, pendulous, axillary flowers, with 3 fused sepals that form a narrow yellowish-green tube with a swollen base, containing the sexual organs; at the tip the tube expands into a broad, rounded limb, up to 4 inches (10 cm) across, purple-brown with white veining; the disagreeable smell attracts pollinating flies and midges. Globose fruit (capsule), opening at base, containing flattened seeds.
Flowering period Midsummer; it flowers continuously and freely on branches of the year.
Cultivation The plant lives in warm climates where the temperature does not fall below 54°F (12°C). It can tolerate short periods at lower temperatures if kept dry. Well-drained, humus-rich soil. Good lighting, especially in winter. Water regularly, more freely in growing period. Prune to shorten at end of winter. Fix an initial support and repot annually in spring. It is prone to attack by red spider mite and whitefly. Because it originates in tropical forests, it may suffer from dry air indoors. Grow in the ground or in a pot.
Propagation In spring by seed or in summer by semiripe cuttings, always under glass.
Use Very delicate, suitable for covering trellises in conservatories.

4   SCHISANDRA RUBIFLORA Rehd. & Wilson

Order Illiciales.
Family Schisandraceae.
Origin China.

Description Branched, compact shrub with stems that twine in pairs. Deciduous, alternate, obovate-lanceolate, dentate leaves. Long-stalked, axillary, solitary, unisexual, deep red flowers, comprising 7 oval parts. Small fruits similar to berries, red, globose, pendulous, arranged along the line of the enlarged, elongated receptacle.
Flowering period Late spring.
Cultivation Half-hardy plant to be grown outdoors; if the temperature is likely to fall to a few degrees above 32°F (0°C), plant in a sheltered spot. Cool soil, not waterlogged. Water regularly. Tolerates full sun but prefers a partially shaded position. Prune normally in winter. Needs staking from the start. Liable to attack by aphids.
Propagation By semiripe cuttings in summer, layering in September, or seed in October.
Use Rapid carpeting plant.

Order Ranunculales.
Family Ranunculaceae.
Origin Southern Europe
(Mediterranean basin).

Description   Herbaceous perennial plant with angular stems, the lower part woody. Deciduous, opposite, slightly coriaceous leaves, bipinnate with 3–5 lanceolate leaflets which remain on the plant until late winter. Small white, scented flowers, formed of 4 linear-oblong sepals, in large, axillary, terminal panicles. Fruit (achene) with feathery tail, in fall.
Flowering period   Late summer.
Cultivation   Hardy plant which adapts well outdoors in temperate climes. Rich, well-drained soil, in sunny position.
Propagation   By layering and air-layering in spring; by semi-ripe cuttings in summer.
Varieties   'Rubella,' with flowers that are red outside; 'Rotundifolia,' with larger leaflets; 'Semiplena,' 'Maritima,' and others.
Use   Grows wild in scrubland of the northern Mediterranean. It can be used as a hedge climber or kept in a pot.

---

6   CLEMATIS MONTANA Buch.–Ham.

Order Ranunculales.
Family Ranunculaceae.
Origin Himalayas.

Description   Vigorous shrub with thin, nodose branches and tendrils. Deciduous, opposite, ovate, ternate leaves with dentate margin. Large, showy, scented, white flowers, tending to turn pink as they fade, numerous on the leaf axil, appearing continuously. Fruit (achene) glabrous with feathered tail.
Flowering period   Spring-summer; on branches of previous year, abundant.
Cultivation   Hardy plant suited to climates with cold winters. Sheltered, averagely sunny sites, but also in shade. Water frequently during summer. Limited pruning because the plant flowers on branches of the previous year, to be done after flowering.
Propagation   By layering and air-layering in spring; by semi-ripe cuttings in summer.
Varieties   'Grandiflora,' very hardy with large pink-white flowers; 'Wilsonii,' white flowers in late summer; 'Rubens,' pink flowers and reddish leaves when young, summer flowering; 'Lilacina,' violet flowers; and others.
Use   Covers broad surfaces in a few years; tends to branch upward.

Order Ranunculales.
Family Ranunculaceae.
Origin China.

Description Perennial, fast-growing climber. Tripinnate leaves, divided into dentate segments. Large, solitary, deep yellow flowers, pendulous and lantern-shaped, on a long peduncle, with 4 pointed, lanceolate sepals.
Flowering period Midsummer to fall; uninterruptedly, on branches of the year.
Cultivation Hardy species, adapting well to temperate climates. Fairly undemanding as to soil and exposure. Prune hard in March; the plant will produce new branches on which flowers will develop in the same year.
Propagation By seed in spring; by semiripe cuttings in summer.
Varieties 'Obtusiuscula,' with smaller, less dentate leaves.
Use The species quickly covers broad surfaces, growing mainly upward.

Order Ranunculales.
Family Ranunculaceae.
Origin Caucasus to Himalayas.

Description Perennial, ramose, rapidly growing climber. Tripinnate, ovate-lanceolate leaves, divided into dentate segments. Campanulate, yellowish flowers with 4 sepals, sometimes reflex, at the tip, solitary or in groups. Gray-silver feathery fruits that remain for a long time on the plant, as in many species of this genus.
Flowering period Late summer; on branches of the year.
Cultivation Hardy plant, suitable for gardens and patios. Easy to grow, it requires cool, drained soil, also flowering in open position or half-shade. Prune at end of winter to stimulate growth of flower branches in spring.
Propagation By semiripe cuttings in summer.
Variety 'Bill Mackenzie,' large yellow flowers.
Use This species, very similar to *C. tangutica*, is much prized for the warm efect of its flowers and the design of its leaves, suitable for filling spaces in greenery.

Order Ranunculales.
Family Ranunculaceae.
Origin Horticultural hybrid, probably *C. lanuginosa x C. viticella*.

Description Shrub with thin, nodose stems. Leaves simple or with 3-5 ovate-acuminate leaflets. Very large, showy, axillary flowers in panicles at tips of branches, long-stalked, violet with 4-6 sepals.

Flowering period Summer-early fall; continuously, on branches of the year.

Cultivation Hardy plant which withstands hard winters, especially if situated in a sheltered, sunny spot, in rich, light soil. Water freely and prune drastically in February to stimulate growth of new flower branches.

Propagation By layering and air-layering; also by semiripe cuttings in summer.

Varieties 'Gipsy Queen,' 'Jackmanii superba,' 'Perle d'Azur,' 'The President,' deep purple flowers and anthers of a different color; 'Duchess of Sutherland,' and 'Rubra,' red flowers; and very many others.

Use This is the most popular garden clematis; excellent for quickly covering any structure. Also does well in a pot.

Order Ranunculales.
Family Ranunculaceae.
Origin Southern Europe.

Description Perennial climber with wooded stem only at the base. Deciduous, tripinnate leaves, mostly divided into 7 lanceolate segments. Solitary, axillary, long-stalked, pendulous, scented flowers, with pink-purple sepals. Spherical infructescence consisting of numerous small uncinate fruits at tip.

Flowering period Summer.

Cultivation Hardy plant that does well in the open in temperate climates. Easy to grow, preferring sunny positions. Prune drastically at end of winter. Also grows well in pots.

Propagation By layering and air-layering in spring; by semiripe cuttings in summer; by seed in fall.

Varieties 'Albiflora,' white flowers; 'Abundance,' light purple flowers; 'Coerulea,' violet-blue flowers; 'Royal Velours,' deep purple flowers; 'Flore Pieno,' double flowers; and others.

Use Also found growing wild in southern Europe; tends to spread rapidly.

Common names
Chocolate vine, Five-leaf akebia.
Order Ranunculales.
Family Lardizabalaceae.
Origin China, Japan, Korea.

Description　Woody, rapid-growing, evergreen twining shrub in climates with mild winters, otherwise deciduous to late fall. Alternate, long-stalked, digitate leaves, composed of 5 ovate-oblong leaflets. Unisexual flowers (monoecious plant), purple-brown, scented, in mixed racemes. Male flowers are smaller and paler than females. Ovoid, purple-brown edible fruits which open when ripe to release black seeds, surrounded by a gelatinous aril. Fruiting is possible when at least two individuals are present because the plant is functionally dioecious.

Flowering period　Late spring.

Cultivation　In cool climates the plant may produce flowers but not fruits; nevertheless it grows well, with abundant foliage. Cool, light, rich, well-drained soil, in sunny or half-shaded position, sheltered from cold winds. Does not tolerate puddles. Tends to lose leaves low down, so pruning of the base is useful at end of flowering period in order to encourage production of new shoots. Not greatly troubled by parasites. Needs support when beginning to grow. It is advisable to thin out and tidy up the climber in winter.

Propagation　Principally by layering at end of winter, but in summer also by semiripe cuttings, or by seed in spring.

Use　Suitable outdoors in temperate zones. Easy to cultivate, it is hardy and undemanding. In countries of origin it is used for infusions.

Opposite: twig with large male flowers and small female flowers. Above: details of flowers and seeds; right: a mature fruit.

12

HOLBOELLIA LATIFOLIA Wall.
Stauntonia latifolia Wall.

Order Ranunculales.
Family Lardizabalaceae.
Origin Himalayas.

Description Rapid-growing shrub with persistent, alternate, long-stalked, digitate leaves with 3–7 ovate, coriaceous, acuminate leaflets. Highly scented, unisexual flowers (monoecious plant) in short axillary racemes, with 6 tiny petaloid sepals and 6 even smaller petals; male flowers greenish, female purplish. Elongated fruits, purple outside with whitish edible pulp, ripe in late fall.

Flowering period Spring.

Cultivation Half-hardy plant which, if planted outdoors, needs a sheltered position and only where the temperature remains above 35°–36°F (2°–3°C); the fruits mature only in a temperate-warm climate. Rich, light, well-drained soil, in sheltered but sunny site. Thin out in summer.

Propagation By semiripe cuttings in early fall; also by seed and layering.

Use Also thrives in pots.

13

MENISPERMUM CANADENSE L.

Common names Canada moonseed, Yellow perilla.
Order Ranunculales.
Family Menispermaceae.
Origin North America.

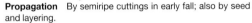

Description Vigorous plant, wooded at base, pubescent when young, with twining stems. Deciduous, stalked leaves, very variable in form, ovate-cordate, with 3–7 barely noticeable or entire lobes, dark green above, light green below. Small, unremarkable, greenish flowers, unisexual (dioecious plant), in long-stalked, loose axillary racemes; 6 sepals and 6 petals. Spherical brown-black fruits, poisonous, with crescent-shaped seeds.

Flowering period Midsummer.

Cultivation Hardy plant that tolerates hard winters outdoors. Fairly sunny position in rich, well-drained soil.

Propagation By root suckers in spring, or by seed.

Use Particularly for covering pergolas, by reason of its much-twined stems.

14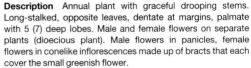

HUMULUS SCANDENS (Lour.) Merr.
H. japonicus Siebold & Zucc.

Common name
Japanese hop.
Order Urticales.
Family Cannabaceae.
Origin Temperate regions
of eastern Asia.

Description Annual plant with graceful drooping stems. Long-stalked, opposite leaves, dentate at margins, palmate with 5 (7) deep lobes. Male and female flowers on separate plants (dioecious plant). Male flowers in panicles, female flowers in conelike inflorescences made up of bracts that each cover the small greenish flower.
Flowering period Late summer.
Cultivation Adapts to any type of fertile, well-drained soil. Tolerates shade but grows better in sunny positions.
Propagation In spring by cuttings of root suckers or directly in the ground by seed.
Varieties 'Variegatus,' with white-tinted or white-streaked leaves; 'Lutescens,' with golden-bronze leaves.
Use Hardy; good for covering trellises and fences.

15 HUMULUS LUPULUS L.

Common names
Common hop, European
hop.
Order Urticales.
Family Cannabaceae.
Origin Europe.

Description Rapid-growing perennial plant with twining, hollow stems covered with uncinate hairs, often twisting around other plants. Long-stalked, opposite, palmate leaves, divided into 3 lobes, dentate at margins. Male and female flowers on separate plants, without petals. Female flowers small, each covered with a bract and joined to form a conical, pendulous, greenish inflorescence which, when the fruits mature, becomes papery. Male flowers greenish, in ramose inflorescences.
Flowering period From late spring to end summer.
Cultivation It adapts well to cold-temperate climates and can, in fact, withstand long periods below 32°F (0°C). Prefers sunny sites but tolerates shade.
Does not require any particular soil and will grow even on clay.
Propagation In spring by apical cuttings and by seed.
Variety 'Aureus,' deep yellow-tinted leaves.
Use Suitable for outdoors, hardy and easy to cultivate, it rapidly covers fences and trellises. In the northern hemisphere it grows wild in woods and hedges. The fruits are used for making beer. The young shoots are edible and can be cooked like asparagus.

Common names
Creeping fig, Climbing fig,
Creeping rubber plant.
Order Urticales.
Family Moraceae.
Origin China and Japan.

Description   Perennial plant; the young stems are slender and provided with clinging roots; these are absent on the mature branches, which do not adhere to the support. Ovate leaves, cordate at the base, small and sessile on the young branches, larger, stalked and shiny on those of a few years old. Inflorescence (syconium) orange, ripening into edible infructescence, variously colored.

Flowering period   Summer.

Cultivation   Grows well in the open in mild climates where the winter temperature does not fall below 41°F (5°C). Well-drained soil, with liberal watering in summer. The plant tends to branch out profusely. Sunny or shady positions. Liable to be attacked by woolly aphids.

Propagation   Cuttings (not easy) of lateral shoots in spring, under glass.

Varieties   'Minima,' smaller leaves, and 'Variegata,' white-streaked leaves.

Use   Half-hardy plant, good for decorative carpeting effects, particularly suitable for covering well-sheltered walls or smooth, vertical surfaces. Does very well in pots.

Common names
Bougainvillea, Paper flower.
Order Caryophyllales.
Family Nyctaginaceae.
Origin Brazil.

Description   Woody plant with strong stems furnished with axillary thorns. Small, deciduous, entire, ovate, shiny leaves. Small yellowish-white tubulous, terminal flowers in groups of 3, each supported by a prominent, ovate, violet bract; the 3 colored bracts may be replaced by a corolla.

Flowering period   Spring-fall.

Cultivation   The plant is sensitive to cold; it grows well in mild climates with temperatures of around 43°–50°F (6°–10°C). Sunny position, in fertile, well-drained soil, even slightly clay. Water moderately, more often in summer, not at all during dormancy. In spring hard-prune branches of previous season. Liable to attack by whitefly. In cooler climates it can be kept in pots, as a shrub, and taken in during the winter.

Propagation   By semiripe cuttings in summer and by hardwood cuttings in winter, both under glass.

Varieties   'Sandarana,' deep violet bracts; 'Snow White,' white bracts with slight green veining; 'Variegata,' deep violet bracts and light-bordered leaves; 'Cipheri,' paler violet bracts.

Use   Half-hardy, very decorative and brightly colored, it is suitable for verandas and conservatories or, in Mediterranean or hot climates, against walls. Easy to cultivate; the most cold-resistant of all bougainvillea species.

18

ERIOCEREUS BONPLANDII (Parm.) Riccob.
Cereus bonplandii Parm.

Order Caryophyllales.
Family Cactaceae.
Origin Brazil.

Description Succulent plant with slender, fleshy, branched stem, and 4–6 wavy-edged wings; there are tufts of spines of about ½ inch (1 cm) in the depressions (areoles), used by the plant for clinging. Solitary, very large, funnel-shaped flowers, up to 8 inches (20 cm), which open at night for a few hours. Edible red fruit (berry), without spines, the white pulp being full of tiny black seeds.
Flowering period Summer-fall.
Cultivation Half-hardy plant that grows well outdoors in a Mediterranean or similar climate with mild winters. Rich, loose soil in sunny position. Water only in summer.
Propagation By stem cuttings and also by seed.
Use It is kept in a pot to obtain more flowers.

19

PERESKIA ACULEATA Mill.

Common names
Barbados gooseberry,
Lemon vine.
Order Caryophyllales.
Family Cactaceae.
Origin Central America.

Description Rapid-growing nonsucculent plant, erect when young, then climbing by means of hooked thorns distributed along the stems. Green branches, with short, curved thorns when young, then brown and woody with tufts of 1–3 straight spines. Deciduous or semievergreen, fleshy, ovate-lanceolate leaves, often with hooked thorns at axil. Large, solitary, scented white flowers in dense panicles, which appear only on plants at least 3 feet (1 m) tall. Light yellow, smooth, edible fruits, the size of an olive.
Flowering period Fall.
Cultivation Delicate climber that can be kept in the open only at temperatures above 50°F (10°C). Water freely during growth period. Soft, well-drained soil, in sunny position. Prune drastically in winter, after leaf fall.
Propagation By semiripe cuttings in summer, by seed under glass in spring.
Varieties 'Godseffiana' and others that differ in the form of leaves and color of flowers.
Use Grows well in pots. In Brazil the leaves are used as infusions. This species belongs to the only genus of nonsucculent cacti, bearing true and proper green leaves, not transformed into spines. For this reason the *Pereskia* species are regarded as primitive members of their family.

20

ANREDERA CORDIFOLIA (Ten.) Steenis
Boussingaultia baselloides H.B.K.

Common names
Madeira vine, Mignonette vine.
Order Caryophyllales.
Family Basellaceae.
Origin South America.

Description Fast-growing perennial climber with twining, semiwooded, reddish stems; tuberous roots. Entire, ovate-lanceolate, slightly fleshy light green leaves. Many small, scented white flowers in panicles of 2–4 inches (5–10 cm), produced at the axil of the upper leaves. Bulbils present at axils of non-flowering leaves. Small indehiscent fruits.
Flowering period September-November.
Cultivation Half-hardy plant, sensitive to frost, at temperatures not below 43°–45°F (6-7C); support necessary. Full light in well-drained, humus-rich soil. Water freely in early stages of growth. In colder climates the entire aerial part of the plant dies with the arrival of the first frosts. Prune the branches of the previous season in spring, even where winters are mild.
Propagation By seed, under glass, in February-March, transplanting in May; also vegetatively with tubers and bulbils.
Use It will grow easily and rapidly to cover supports, trellises, and pergolas.

21

BASELLA RUBRA L.

Common name Malabar spinach
Order Caryophyllales.
Family Basellaceae.
Origin Tropical regions of Asia and Africa.

Description Herbaceous perennial plant with fleshy stems. Deciduous, alternate, fleshy leaves, very variable in form, usually cordate, almost entire. Red or pink flowers in loose spikes.
Flowering period Delicate hothouse plant which can be kept indoors and transferred outside at the end of May. In temperate climates it is usually grown as an annual or a biennial. Averagely sunny position in rich, cool soil. Needs a support.
Propagation In March by seed, under glass, to go outside in May; also by cuttings.
Variety 'Alba,' white flowers.
Use Once it was grown as an edible plant, its leaves used like spinach. Today it is essentially decorative.

Common name Berry catchfly.
Order Caryophyllales.
Family Caryophyllaceae.
Origin Europe, western Asia.

Description   Herbaceous perennial plant with slender, prostrate, ascendant and drooping stems that spread very widely. The opposite, ovate-elliptic leaves are more or less pointed, while those of the inflorescences are narrower (bracts). The flowers are curious, in large, sparse panicles, with 5 whitish petals, deeply bifid, narrow and folded briefly above the calyx. Shiny black fruit (berry), pea-sized, containing numerous small black seeds.

Flowering period   Summer.

Cultivation   Hardy plant, easy to cultivate. Needs cool, preferably rich, soil; tolerates some humidity. Grows well even in shade.

Propagation   By seed in late summer and fall; also by cuttings in summer.

Use   Although it grows to some length, this is not a species to provide cover and it is best to let it climb among other plants. It can also be planted along river banks and on embankments.

Common names Coral vine, Mexican creeper.
Order Polygonales.
Family Polygonaceae.
Origin Mexico.

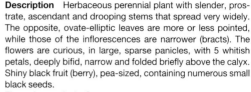

Description   Very sturdy perennial plant with slender stems and tendrils at the tips of the inflorescence; edible tuberous roots. The ovate-cordate leaves are persistent in tropical regions. Small deep pink flowers, without petals, made up of 5 sepals (3 large and 2 narrower), in axillary racemes or terminal panicles.

Flowering period   Late spring to early fall, plentifully and continuously on branches of the year; year-round in regions of origin.

Cultivation   This climber from tropical and subtropical zones grows well where the temperature does not fall below 50°F (10°C). Fertile, well-drained soil. Water and feed freely during growth phase. Prune at the end of winter.

Propagation   By cuttings or by seed in summer; also by layering.

Varieties   'Album,' white flowers; there are also cultivars with double flowers.

Use   Delicate plant, needing to be raised in the conservatory or temperate greenhouse; can be brought outside in good weather. It needs large containers because of its extensive root development. The beauty of the foliage is much appreciated.

Common names Mile-a-minute plant, Russian vine.
Order Polygonales.
Family Polygonaceae.
Origin Western China and Tibet.

Description Fast-growing woody plant. Large, stalked, deciduous, ovate-lanceolate leaves. Small, campanulate white or greenish-white flowers, in elongated panicles at tips of branches.
Flowering period Summer-fall.
Cultivation Hardy plant suitable for temperate climates, where it grows well in the open. Sunny sites encourage abundant flowering. Cool, well-drained, preferably rich soil. Water frequently. Prune often to restrict excessive growth.
Propagation By softwood cuttings in summer; seldom produces seeds.
Use Rapidly covers large surfaces. It closely resembles *Polygonum baldschuanicum*. It is a fairly aggressive plant which in many parts of the world has escaped from cultivation, finding its way into natural vegetation, where it tends to form almost impenetrable thickets.

25 PLUMBAGO AURICULATA Lam.
P. capensis Thunb.

Common name Cape leadwort.
Order Plumbaginales.
Family Plumbaginaceae.
Origin South Africa.

Description Woody shrub or herbaceous annual plant, drooping and partially climbing, showing rapid growth. Alternate, ovate, short-stalked leaves, persistent only in warmer climates. Tubulous, terminal, deep blue flowers, with a long, slender corolline tube, 5-lobed, in somewhat contracted, umbrella-shaped spikes.
Flowering period Summer-fall; freely and continuously, on branches of the year.
Cultivation Grows well outside where the temperature does not fall below 34°–45°F (1°–7°C), but tolerates short frosts. In regions with colder winters, mulch the base and later cover with polythene. Bright but sheltered site; cool soil, not waterlogged. Water regularly, thinning out in winter. In spring hard-prune the previous year's branches. If grown as a climber, it needs support, otherwise it tends to form a drooping shrub.
Propagation By cuttings in spring-summer; by seed in spring (but flowers the following year); by division of large clumps, before flowering, in spring; also by layering.
Use Half-hardy. It can be grown in large pots on sheltered patios in a Mediterranean climate, and also on balconies and in conservatories.

26

ACTINIDIA CHINENSIS Planch.

Common names Kiwi fruit, Chinese gooseberry.
Order Theales.
Family Actinidiaceae.
Origin Northern and eastern China, alongside watercourses.

Description   Fast-growing perennial plant with strong woody stems, up to 33 feet (10 m) long. Deciduous, obovate-rounded leaves with undulate margins and distanced teeth. Slightly scented unisexual or bisexual flowers with 5–6 creamy white petals, later turning brown at margins. Edible fruit (rich in vitamin C) with characteristic pubescent rind, maturing in late fall. The plant is functionally dioecious, bearing both male and female flowers, but also bisexual flowers. To obtain fruit it is necessary to grow female plants near a male plant.
Flowering period   Late spring.
Cultivation   A temperate-cold-climate plant which can withstand cold winters in the open. Prefers a sunny site, well sheltered from wind. Soil should always be cool (water freely) but not waterlogged. Hard-prune at end of winter. The plant is unlikely to be affected by disease.
Propagation   Normally by semiripe cuttings, in late summer, but also by seed in spring.
Varieties   'Hayward,' 'Jones,' 'Greensil,' 'Allison,' and 'Abbott.'
Use   Suitable for pergolas. Because of its extensive surface root system, it is unsuitable for growing in pots.

27

ACTINIDIA KOLOMIKTA (Maxim. & Rupr.) Maxim.

Order Theales.
Family Actinidiaceae.
Origin China, Japan, and Korea, where it often forms impenetrable thickets.

Description   Perennial shrub with long woody stems of up to 10 feet (3 m), often twined in pairs. The deciduous, ovate-oblong leaves turn whit or pink after exposure to the sun but tend in the course of the season to fade. Small, scented, unisexual or bisexual flowers with 5–6 white petals, often hidden by the leaves; yellow anthers. Small, edible yellow fruit which ripens in September, with smooth rind. The plant is functionally dioecious, i.e. although bearing hermaphrodite flowers, it behaves either as male or female; it is necessary to have female and male plants in order to produce fruit.
Flowering period   Late spring.
Cultivation   Very hardy plant which withstands hard frosts and is therefore adapted to temperate-cold climes. It prefers sunny positions but also grows well in the shade. Even tolerates clay soils. The plant tends to form clumps if the branches are not guided and fixed, and to spread: if space is limited, prune the branches in February. Otherwise prune moderately (unlike *A. chinensis*). It is not subject to disease or parasite attacks, but it does attract cats who may damage the stems.
Propagation   By semiripe cuttings in August or by seed in spring.
Use   Very suitable for pergolas and trellis-covered walls, due to its dense, colored foliage.

Common name Pitcher plant.
Order Nepenthales.
Family Nepenthaceae.
Origin Southeast Asia.

Description Herbaceous perennial plant, lianoid, insectivorous, with woody base. The leaves are of two types. The first form basal rosettes and are lanceolate, the tip prolonged into a tendril and terminating in a curious pitcher (ascidium) with a lid (operculum); it is light green, often spotted red. The others have tendrils but no ascidia. The flowers are white, unisexual (dioecious plant), without petals but with 4 sepals, in elongated racemes.
Flowering period Summer.
Cultivation This species from warm-humid tropical regions can be grown in temperate zones only in a hothouse where the temperature is always kept at over 68°F (20°C). Bright position but not in direct sun. High air humidity (spray the leaves). Cool, light and well-drained soil, never calcareous; does best in cool, acid peat. Prune the upper branches lightly (the ascidia appear more frequently on the lower branches). Never use calcareous water; demineralized water is best.
Propagation By cuttings in summer in very humid surroundings at a temperature of 77°F (25°C), or by seed in spring.
Use Much more commonly available are *Nepenthes* hybrids, suitable for growing in pots. Secreted inside the ascidia is a sticky liquid that attracts small insects which, having fallen into the trap, are digested by the leaves.

Common name Coral plant.
Order Violales.
Family Flacourtiaceae.
Origin Central China, now probably extinct in the wild.

Description Perennial shrub with thin, semitwining stems. Persistent, alternate, stalked leaves, ovate-cordate, shiny, coriaceous, spinulose-dentate. Globose, long-stalked, pendulous red flowers in terminal racemes. Fruit (berry) rare in cultivated plants.
Flowering period Summer.
Cultivation Grows well outside in temperate climates, but better if against a wall and heltered from the wind. Loose, humus-rich soil, neutral to acid. Water very freely; in regions of origin the rainfall exceeds 80 inches (2000 mm) a year. Prune at end of winter. Needs a support.
Propagation By semiripe cuttings in spring, but also in fall; by seed in spring; by layering in fall.
Use Hardy plant which can be grown in a pot; in winter, when temperatures are very low, it should be brought indoors.

Common name
Common passionflower,
Blue passionflower.
Order Violales.
Family Passifloraceae.
Origin Tropical regions of
South America.

Description Rapid-growing perennial plant with woody stems and axillary tendrils. Semievergreen, palmate leaves with 5–7 deeply incised lobes. The spectacular long-stalked flowers have 5 sepals and 5 white or pinkish alternate petals. Inside the corolla is a halo of filaments (corona) with colored transverse bands. In the center is a protruding structure that bears 5 hammer-shaped stamens and 3 stigmas. The yellow-orange ovoid fruit (berry) is very decorative and matures at the end of summer.

Flowering period From June to September it produces an abundance of flowers on shoots of the year.

Cultivation A sunny position and moderate feeding guarantee a long flowering season. Too much feeding causes luxuriant leaf growth at the expense of flower production. Although it is one of the hardiest of passion flowers, it cannot tolerate intense cold; in temperate-warm climates it can be cultivated outdoors but seldom withstands harsh winters with temperatures around 32°F (0°C). The plant should be supported by a stake when it starts to grow; when it finishes flowering, the excess branches should be eliminated by pruning. In harsh climates, at the end of winter, the plant regrows from the base.

Propagation By hardwood cuttings in spring-summer, or by seed under glass.

Variety 'Constance Elliott,' with bigger and entirely white flowers, is hardier than the type species.

Use Half-hardy plant that does well in pots, suitable for patios, especially in festoons. In cold climates bring indoors in winter, at 46°–50°F (8°–10°C) or cover with polythene.

Flowering twig with tendrils. The yellow-orange ovoid fruit matures in late summer.

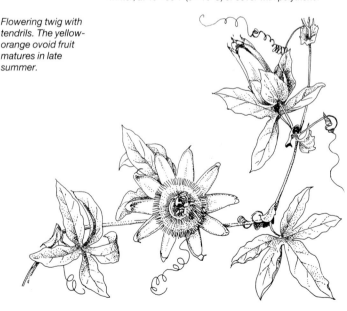

31

PASSIFLORA QUADRIGLANDULOSA
Rodschied

Common names
Granadilla, Giant granadilla.
Order Violales.
Family Passifloraceae.
Origin Tropical South America.

Description Perennial plant with sturdy woody stems covered in thick reddish down. Tendrils present. Ovate leaves, slightly dentate at margin. Showy bright red flowers of 3–4 inches (7–10 cm) with 5 sepals and 5 similar petals. Small threadlike corona, in the center of which is the gynophore, bearing stamens and stigmas.

Flowering period Midsummer.

Cultivation Does not tolerate frost and can be grown outside only in climates where the temperature does not fall below 59°F (15°C). Plant in well-drained soil, watering freely during summer. As with all passion flowers, the leaves are liable to be attacked by the cucumber mosaic virus.

Propagation By hardwood cuttings in summer; by seed, under glass, in spring.

Use Delicate plant with a root apparatus that does not require much space; it can be grown in a large container and brought inside during the winter. Good for covering trellises.

32

PASSIFLORA MOLLISSIMA (H.B.K.) Bailey
Tacsonia mollissima H.B.K.

Common names Curuba, Banana passion fruit.
Order Violales.
Family Passifloraceae.
Origin Tropical South America.

Description Fast-growing, strong-stemmed perennial plant with tendrils. Palmate leaves with 3 deep lobes, finely dentate at margin. The tubulous, pendent, deep pink flowers, 3–3½ inches (7–8 cm) across, are borne singly on long stalks at the leaf axils. The oblong fruit (berry), yellowish when ripe, contains a very large number of seeds wrapped in a yellowish mucilaginous aril, and is edible.

Flowering period June to October.

Cultivation The plant can be grown outside only in mild climates where the temperature does not fall below 10°C (50°F) and does best in a well-sheltered position, against a wall, or otherwise in a greenhouse; also in averagely big pots. Loose, well-drained soil, with fertilizer only in spring. Water plentifully during summer. Prune by thinning out at the end of winter. Plants damaged by frost often regrow from the base. The leaves may exhibit yellow spots among the veins as a result of viruses.

Propagation By hardwood cuttings in summer; by seed, under glass, in spring.

Use Delicate plant that climbs freely over wires and wall trellises.

33

CUCURBITA FICIFOLIA C.D. Bouché
C. melanosperma A. Braun

Common names
Malabar gourd, Fig-leaf gourd.
Order Violales.
Family Cucurbitaceae.
Origin Central America.

Description   Perennial plant with delicate stems that tend to become woody, covered in sharp bristles; axillary tendrils. Large, long-stalked, alternate leaves, ovate-cordate with 5 lobes, sometimes spotted. The deep yellow axillary, bell-shaped flowers are unisexual (monoecious plant), the males long-stalked. Large, heavy, ovoid fruit with a hard rind, containing yellowish-white threadlike soda pulp; black seeds.
Flowering period   Late spring-summer.
Cultivation   In temperate climates the plant is grown as an annual. Cool, rich soil, in sunny position. Water freely and provide with a strong stake to support the weight of fruit.
Propagation   By seed in spring.
Variety   'Mexicana', with bigger seeds. Other members of the genus include the winter squash (*C. maxima*), the warty squash (*C. moschata*) and the summer squash (*C. pepo*), all grown for edible purposes.
Use   Easy to cultivate, the plant produces an abundance of fruit that can be eaten after being boiled.

34

SECHIUM EDULE (Jacq.) Sw.

Common names
Chayote, Choyote, Christophine.
Order Violales.
Family Cucurbitaceae.
Origin Indonesia and Australia.

Description   Perennial climber with tuberous roots, slender, angular stems, and ramose tendrils. Persistent, stalked, digitate leaves with 3–5 deep lobes, entire or with crenate, waxy margin. Unisexual whitish flowers (monoecious plant) with pointed, fringed petals, opening at night; female flowers soiltary, males in large racemes on a long peduncle without bracts. Fruits initially green with white stripes, then orange, in various shapes and sizes.
Flowering period   Midsummer.
Cultivation   Tropical plant which is raised as an annual in temperate climes. Grow against a south-facing wall in sunny position, in loose, cool, rich soil. Water freely.
Propagation   By seed, under glass, in March, bringing outside in May.
Use   The plant is easy to grow and valued for its foliage, fringed flowers and brightly colored fruits. In its original countries the unripe fruit is eaten; when ripe it is fibrous and bitter.

35

CYCLANTHERA PEDATA Schrad.

Order Violales.
Family Cucurbitaceae.
Origin Mexico.

Description Sturdy, fast-growing perennial plant which clings by means of bifid tendrils. Deciduous, cordate leaves with 5–7 sharply dentate lobes. Small, yellowish, unisexual flowers (monoecious plant), the males in racemes. Greenish fruits with darker veins, smooth or with soft spines, with spongy soda pulp and black seeds. When mature, the fruits burst open.
Flowering period Summer.
Cultivation In temperate climates it is cultivated as an annual. Sunny, sheltered site; soft, rich, cool, well-drained soil. To obtain fruits it is best grown in a temperate greenhouse.
Propagation By seed, under glass, in early spring; transplant in May.
Use Easy to cultivate. In original countries the unripe fruits are pickled and eaten like cucumbers.

36

LAGENARIA SICERARIA Standl.
L. Leucantha Rusby, *L. vulgaris* Ser.

Common name White-flowered gourd.
Order Violales.
Family Cucurbitaceae.
Origin Probably Africa, possibly India.

Description Annual herbaceous plant, fast-growing especially in warm climates, with thin, pubescent stems and ramose tendrils. Large, deciduous, alternate leaves, broadly ovate, sometimes with 3–7 long-stalked, cordate lobes, slightly pubescent underneath. Large, showy white flowers, unisexual (usually monoecious, rarely dioecious plant), on long peduncles, in racemes; they last only for one day. Fruit variable but quite large, elongated, pendulous, swollen at base, with a green or white-streaked rind which becomes woody; ripens in fall.
Flowering period Spring.
Cultivation Hardy plant which can be grown outside even in temperate climes. Well-drained, fairly rich, loose soil in sunny but sheltered position. Water plentifully. Needs strong support; while ripening, the fruit should be raised above ground so that the base is not flattened.
Propagation By seed in spring.
Varieties There are various cultivars that differ in the shape of fruit.
Use The plant, easy to grow, has a musky odor that for some people may be disagreeable. Thanks to the luxuriant foliage, it is suitable for covering fences and trellises. In its original countries the fruits are eaten but used above all, after drying and scraping, to make containers. They are also used as musical instruments.

37   LUFFA AEGYPTIACA Mill.
L. cylindrica Roem.

Common names Loofah, Sponge gourd.
Order Violales.
Family Cucurbitaceae.
Origin Tropical regions of Africa and Asia.

Description Sturdy annual herbaceous plant with long stems bearing multifid tendrils. Deciduous, long-stalked, palmate leaves of 5–7 dentate lobes, rough on both sides. Large, yellow, axillary, unisexual flowers (monoecious plant), the females short-stalked and solitary, the males larger, in long-stalked racemes. Cylindrical-clavate fruits, smooth and edible, with black seeds.
Flowering period Summer.
Cultivation Can be grown outside even in temperate climates, preferably against a wall. Cool, rich, loose soil, in sunny but sheltered position. Water freely. In temperate zones plants grown outdoors seldom produce fruit unless there is a particularly long summer and high air humidity.
Propagation By seed in spring, bringing outside in May.
Use Delicate and demanding plant. In original countries the unripe fruit is eaten; while ripening it develops strong fibers that constitutes the sponge or loofah.

38   MOMORDICA CHARANTIA L.

Common names Balsam pear, La-kwa, Bitter gourd, Bitter cucumber.
Order Violales.
Family Cucurbitaceae.
Origin Tropical regions of Asia and Africa.

Description Annual herbaceous plant with much-branched stems and many delicate tendrils, simple and opposed to the leaves. The deciduous, long-stalked, alternate leaves are palmate-cordate with 5–7 lobes and rounded sinuses, sometimes with dentate margins, colored dull green. Small, axillary, yellow flowers, unisexual (monoecious plant), made up of 5 sepals and 5 petals; the females are always solitary, sthen orange, dehiscent through 3 valves when mature, containing flattened dark seeds, wrapped inside an edible red aril.
Flowering period Summer.
Cultivation In temperate climates it grows outside and completes its entire vegetative cycle between spring and fall. Rich, cool, loose soil, watering frequently. Grows well both in full sun and shade.
Propagation By seed, under glass or in a seedbed, in early spring, bringing out in May.
Variety 'Abbreviata,' with narrower lobes and fruit with rows of spines; according to some authors, it is a distinct species.
Use Especially for covering fences and trellises. The fruit is edible when still unripe (must be cooked, otherwise bitter).

39

TRICHOSANTHES CUCUMEROIDES
Maxim. ex Franch. & Sav.

Order Violales.
Family Cucurbitaceae.
Origin Indonesia and
Australia.

Description   Perennial climber with tuberous roots and slender, angular stems; ramose tendrils. Persistent, stalked leaves, digitate with 3–5 deep lobes, entire or with crenulate, waxy margin. Unisexual flowers (monoecious plant), red with long-fringed, pointed petals, opening at night; the females are solitary, the males in large racemes, borne on a long stalk without a bract. The fruit is initially green with white streaks, then orange, in various shapes and sizes.
Flowering period   Midsummer.
Cultivation   Tropical plant which is grown as an annual in temperate climes. Does well against a south-facing wall. Loose, cool, rich soil, in sunny position. Water plentifully.
Propagation   By seed, under glass, in March, then bring outside in May.
Use   Easy to cultivate, the plant is valued for its foliage, fringed flowers and brightly colored fruit. In original countries the unripe fruit is eaten, becoming fibrous and bitter when mature.

40

BRYONIA DIOICA Jacq.

Common names Red
bryony, Wild hop.
Order Violales.
Family Cucurbitaceae.
Origin Europe.

Description   Fast-growing herbaceous perennial plant with twining annual stems that bear axillary tendrils; large, tuberous roots. Deciduous, alternate leaves, palmate-lobate with 5 fairly pointed lobes and a cordate base. Unisexual greenish-white flowers (dioecious plant) in axillary racemes, the males somewhat bigger than the females. Globose fruit (berry), initially green, then red.
Flowering period   Late spring-summer.
Cultivation   Hardy plant, easy to cultivate. Grows easily in any soil provided it is not too dry, and preferably rich. Develops a large fleshy root that produces new shoots every year. Fairly sunny position.
Propagation   By seed in fall or by root cuttings in summer.
Use   Because of its hardy habit and rapid growth rate it can be used as an annual cover for trellises and pergolas. Grows wild in scrubland and hedges of southern Europe.

Order Rosales.
Family Pittosporaceae.
Origin Southeast
Australia.

Description Woody plant with stems that twine in pairs. The aromatic leaves are persistent, alternate, narrowly lanceolate and coriaceous. The small bell-shaped flowers are pendulous, solitary and axillary, at the tips of the branches, with 5 petals that are initially greenish-yellow, then tinted purple. The bluish-purple fruit (berry), about the size of an olive, matures in fall and is edible.

Flowering period Summer.

Cultivation Half-hardy plant which cannot withstand hard frosts and intense cold but grows well in cool, humid climates. Well-drained, cool, fairly rich, loose soil, neutral to acid, in fairly sunny, sheltered site. Water more plentifully in summer. Prune to shape in spring.

Propagation By seed in spring; by semiripe cuttings in summer.

Varieties Numerous cultivars with larger flowers and red or white fruits.

Use A fairly compact climber, suitable for patios. The fruits are similar to blueberries.

Details of plant, which has small, drooping, solitary, bell-shaped flowers and long bluish fruits, the size of an olive.

Right: edible fruits
provide a colorful fall
display.

Common name Climbing hydrangea.
Order Rosales.
Family Hydrangeaceae.
Origin Japan.

Description Vigorous climbing shrub with stems that branch from the base and climb by means of clinging roots. Long-stalked, deciduous, opposite leaves, broadly ovate-cordate, pointed, and dentate. Small hermaphroditic, monoclamid flowers, creamy-white, in a flattened, terminal corymb; the fertile flowers are surrounded by a few large, persistent sterile flowers, comprising 4 conspicuous, whitish petaloid sepals, designed to attract pollinators. The fruit (capsule) has a residue of the calyx at the tip (inferior ovary).

Flowering period Summer; very abundant, on previous year's branches.

Cultivation Hardy plant, very adaptable to cold-temperate climates. Cool, rich, well-drained, moderately acid soil, in shady or fairly sunny positions. Water very frequently, preferably with lime-free water, to keep the soil moist. Prune lightly.

Propagation By semiripe cuttings in summer or by softwood cuttings in spring, under glass; alternatively by layering in spring.

Use Particularly for covering shaded walls. Not to be confused with *Schizophragma hydrangeoides*, the sterile flowers of which each have only one sepal.

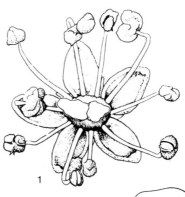

1

Right: 1. fertile flower, much enlarged; 2. sterile flower, with just four large sepals. The typical appearance of the inflorescence depends on the presence and distribution of both types of flower.

2

43 PILEOSTEGIA VIBURNOIDES Hook. & Thoms.
Schizophragma viburnoides (Hook. & Thoms.) Stapf

Order Rosales.
Family Hydrangeaceae.
Origin Himalayas and eastern Asia.

Description Vigorous woody plant with stems that bear numerous clinging roots. Evergreen, opposite, ovate-lanceolate, coriaceous leaves, with raised veins on the lower side. Small whitish flowers of 4–5 petals, hemaphroditic, in terminal, flattened corymb.
Flowering period Late summer-early fall.
Cultivation Hardy plant which does well outdoors in temperate climes. Shelter against a wall in zones where winters are harsh. Light, well-drained, preferably rich soil, in fairly sunny positions. Water freely, especially in summer. Prune in spring.
Propagation By semiripe cuttings in late summer or by softwood cuttings in spring.
Use Good carpeting plant for west-facing walls. It is distinguished from the genus *Schizophragma* by its evergreen leaves and from the genus *Hydrangea* by the absence of sterile flowers.

44 SCHIZOPHRAGMA HYDRANGEOIDES Siebold & Zucc.

Common name
Japanese hydrangea vine.
Order Rosales.
Family Hydrangeaceae.
Origin Japan.

Description Strong climber with woody stems and clinging roots. Deciduous, opposite, cordate, broadly ovate, deeply dentate, thin-stalked leaves, often reddish, dark above and blue-gray below. Small, whitish, hermaphroditic flowers, surrounded by larger, sterile, creamy white flowers, consisting of a single broadly ovate sepal (a distinctive feature of the genus), in large, flattened terminal corymbs.
Flowering period Summer.
Cultivation Hardy plant that does well in the open, even in cooler climates. Rich, cool, moderately acid soil, in shady or fairly sunny position. Water freely in summer. Prune to keep tidy in fall or spring.
Propagation By semiripe cuttings in summer; by layering in fall; by air-layering in summer.
Variety 'Roseum,' with pink-tinted sterile flower sepals.
Use Quickly forms a carpet, but also good for north-facing walls. Does very well in shady gardens and parks.

Order Rosales.
Family Rosaceae.
Origin Northern China.

Description Rampant climbing rose, fast-growing, with strong stems and a few hooked thorns. The leaves are composed of 5–7 ovate-lanceolate, glabrous, dentate leaflets, glandulous on lower side. Cup-shaped, scented, creamy white flowers in dense panicles; deciduous sepals.
Flowering season Summer.
Cultivation Hardy species that needs a sunny position and well-drained soil.
Propagation By cuttings or by grafting.
Variety 'Kiftsgate,' masses of white flowers.
Use With its light, luxuriant foliage, it is ideal for covering walls and pergolas.

Common name Cherokee rose.
Order Rosales.
Family Rosaceae.
Origin China and Taiwan to Burma.

Description Vigorous shrub with smooth green stems and curved thorns. Persistent, coriaceous, ternate leaves with shiny, ovate, dentate leaflets. Large, scented, solitary white flowers; persistent sepals. Rough, red false fruit (hip).
Flowering period Very prolifically in summer.
Cultivation Half-hardy plant that can live outdoors only in climates with mild winters because it cannot withstand frosts. Fairly compact, cool, rich (even slightly calcareous) soil, in warm, sunny position. Water plentifully in summer. Needs staking.
Propagation By semiripe cuttings, grafting, or seed.
Use Against well-exposed fences and walls.

47

ROSA BANKSIAE Ait. f.

Order Rosales.
Family Rosaceae.
Origin China.

Description Rampant climbing shrub with thin, branching stems, almost without thorns. Semievergreen, alternate leaves, composed of 3–5 shiny lanceolate leaflets, narrow at the tip, dentate margins. Slightly scented, white flowers, 1¼–1½ inches (3–4 cm), in large corymbous panicles. Globose red false fruit (hip).

Flowering period Spring, on previous year's branches.

Cultivation Hardy plant that adapts to temperate-cold climates and will even tolerate some frost, particularly if grown against a well-exposed wall. Rich, compact, well-drained, even calcareous soil. It flowers most freely in sunny, sheltered positions. Prune after flowering and remove dry branches. Liable to attack by aphids. Needs staking.

Propagation By hardwood cuttings in fall, by grafting or by air-layering in early summer.

Varieties 'Alba,' single white flowers; 'Alba Plena,' double white flowers; 'Lutescens,' single yellow flowers; 'Lutea,' double flowers.

Use Easy to cultivate; can also be grown in pots.

48

ROSA SEMPERVIRENS L.

Common name
Evergreen rose.
Order Rosales.
Family Rosaceae.
Origin Mediterranean area.

Description Vigorous, spreading, climbing shrub with strong, curving thorns. Shiny evergreen leaves, made up of 5–7 ovate-acuminate leaflets, with sharply dentate margins. Inflorescence of 3–7 white flowers with deciduous sepals.

Flowering period Late spring.

Cultivation Hardy plant, but does not tolerate particularly long, intense periods of frost. Sunny position, in well-drained soil.

Propagation By semiripe cuttings in spring.

Use Decorative for walls and fences.

49

CLIANTHUS PUNICEUS Banks & Sol.
Donia punicea G. Don

Common names Parrot's bill, Glory pea.
Order Fabales.
Family Fabaceae.
Origin New Zealand.

Description Semicreeping plant with weak, drooping, branched stems. Evergreen, alternately paripinnate leaves with 10–12 pairs of shiny, ovate, short-stalked, coriaceous leaflets. The large bright red flowers look slightly papilionaceous (the wings not covering the keel) and form small, pendulous, axillary, long-stalked racemes at the tips of the branches; the keel is elongated, falciform, with short wings and a backward-folding vexillum.

Flowering period Late spring-summer; abundant on previous year's branches.

Cultivation Half-hardy plant that does not tolerate frost. It can be grown outside only in warmer climates, in sunny, sheltered positions, otherwise indoors or in a temperate greenhouse, bringing out in late May. Outdoors it tends to lose its leaves in fall, Well-drained, light and fairly rich soil. Prune to shorten after flowering. Do not water in winter. Needs a support because of its creeping tendency.

Propagation By seed in early spring, under glass, to flower after two years; by semisoftwood cuttings in summer.

Varieties 'Albus,' creamy white flowers; 'Magnificus,' larger leaves and flowers; 'Roseus,' pink flowers; also cultivars with bicolored flowers.

Use Easy to cultivate and also suitable for pots because of its modest size of 3–5 feet (1–1.5 m). Delicate foliage.

50

CLITORIA TERNATEA L.
Ternatea vulgaris H.B.K.

Common name Butterfly pea.
Order Fabales.
Family Fabaceae.
Origin Indonesia (Ternate Island)

Description Suffruticous plant with numerous graceful stems, pubescent when young. imparipinnate, with 5 soft, ovate, short-stalked leaflets; persistent stipules. The solitary, showy, papilionaceous, stalked, axillary flower is bluish with an erect vexillum, wavy margin and narrow base, very short, spreading wings and a curved, pointed keel.

Flowering period Late spring-summer.

Cultivation Half-hardy plant, to be grown in the open only in temperate-warm climates. Loose, light, well-drained soil, in south-facing, sheltered site. Water plentifully in summer, sparingly in winter.

Propagation By seed or hardwood cuttings, under glass.

Varieties 'Alba,' white flowers; 'Coerulea,' 'Major,' 'Flore Pleno.'

Use Very beautiful climber, both for flowers and leaves. Easy to grow in pots; transfer to greenhouse in winter.

51 DOLICHOS LABLAB L.

Common name Australian pea, Hyacinth bean.
Order Fabales.
Family Fabaceae.
Origin Tropical regions of Asia.

Description Fast-growing perennial herbaceous plant with branching, twining stems. Deciduous ternate leaves with 3 broadly ovate, stalked, cuneate, acuminate, scabrous leaflets, green with violet veining. Large, scented, papilionaceous, purplish flowers in erect axillary racemes of 3-8 blooms, with a curved keel (unlike *Phaseolus*). Flat, elongated fruit (legume) with undulate margin, surmounted by remains of calyx. Seeds are variable in color, white, yellowish, black, often flushed red.
Flowering period Summer.
Cultivation Half-hardy plant that does well outdoors even in areas with mild winters, but will not tolerate frost. Cultivated form is grown as an annual. Well-drained soil of any type, even poor, in sunny or fairly sunny positions. Withstands drought well, but abundant watering favors better flower production.
Propagation By seed in early spring.
Varieties 'Giganteus,' more vigorous with larger white flowers; 'Alba,' white flowers; 'Purpurea,' violet leaves, flowers, and legumes.
Use Climber cultivated since ancient times in tropical parts of the Old World for its seeds and edible legumes. Easy to grow, it does well in pots and will rapidly cover well-exposed pergolas and trellises.

52 HARDENBERGIA COMPTONIANA Benth.

Order Fabales.
Family Fabaceae.
Origin Western Australia.

Description Woody-based climber with graceful, flat, branching, much twisted stems. Persistent stalked leaves composed of 3–5 ovate-lanceolate leaflets, obtuse, truncate at the base. Small, papilionaceous, blue-violet flowers, paired or in groups of 3–4 blooms in long, loose, axillary, terminal racemes. Straight, swollen fruit (legume).
Flowering period Winter-early spring.
Cultivation Half-hardy plant that lives outside in temperate climes where the winter temperature remains at about 44°F (7°C). At rather lower temperatures, plant against a wall or cover with plastic in winter. Well-drained, manured soil, in sunny position. Water in summer and while flowering. Prune at end of winter.
Propagation By semiripe cuttings in late summer; by seed (soaked in water for a time) in spring; always under glass.
Varieties Cultivars with white or pink flowers.
Use Modest-sized climber, suitable for warm patios or conservatories.

Common name Sweet pea.
Order Fabales.
Family Leguminosae.
Origin Southern Italy and Sicily, dry wasteland.

Description Annual herbaceous plant of fairly rapid growth, soon reaching 6½ feet (2 m); graceful winged stems. Deciduous, alternate leaves made up of 2 ovate leaflets and terminating in a branching tendril. Large, papilionaceous, scented flowers in long-stalked racemes of 1–3 blooms; corolla with purple vexillum, wings and violet keel. Elongated fruit (legume).
Flowering period Spring-summer.
Cultivation Plant that is well adapted to temperate climes, preferring sunny positions. Cool, loose, manured, well-drained and slightly alkaline soil. Water more often in growing phase. Feed plentifully until flowers appear. Needs a support. Remove faded flowers to achieve continuous flowering. Prune young plants to develop side shoots.
Propagation By seed in fall or spring, in the ground; the seedlings can withstand cold spring days. Immerse the seeds in warm water to accelerate germination.
Varieties There are hundreds of cultivars, variously colored, of different size and with different flowering times, with more prolific racemes. There are also nonclimbing dwarf forms.
Use Easy to cultivate, this is also suitable for patios; grown for cut flowers.

Order Fabales.
Family Leguminosae.
Origin Mediterranean area.

Description Annual herbaceous plant with slightly winged stems. Deciduous leaves, the lower ones reduced simply to a winged stalk, the upper ones with 3–4 pairs of straight leaflets, terminating in a branched tendril. Papilionaceous flowers with a red vexillum and violet-blue wings, solitary or in racemes of 2–6.
Flowering period Spring.
Cultivation Grows well in temperate climes. Sunny position, in cool, well-drained soil. Water freely during early development phase. Needs a support.
Propagation By seed (previously soaked in warm water) in spring or fall.
Use Easy to cultivate, suitable for patios but not good for cover.

Common names Everlasting pea, Perennial pea
Order Fabales.
Family Leguminosae
Origin Europe.

Description Fast-growing perennial herbaceous plant with winged stems. Deciduous leaves composed of 2 leaflets, dark green above, blue-gray below, ovate, mucronate, terminating in branched tendrils; 2 large stipules. Large papilionaceous violet-red flowers, in racemes of 5–15. Fruit (legume) with 10–12 seeds.

Flowering period Late spring-summer.

Cultivation Hardy species that does well in temperate climates with cold winters. Undemanding as to soil, provided it is not too heavy; in nature it also grows in sandy soil. Water freely during growth phase. Needs staking. The plant spreads sideways.

Propagation After soaking the seeds in warm water, setting them outside in fall. Also by division of clumps in spring.

Varieties 'White Pearl' and 'Snow Queen,' white flowers.

Use Also does well in pots. Suitable as a subject for covering low fences, hedges, and so on. Grows wild in Mediterranean, in wasteland and hedgerows, often in sandy, dry soil.

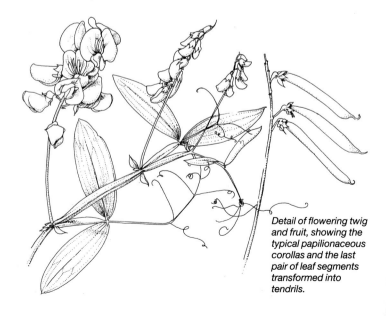

Detail of flowering twig and fruit, showing the typical papilionaceous corollas and the last pair of leaf segments transformed into tendrils.

56 PUERARIA LOBATA (Willd.) Ohwi
P. thunbergiana (Siebold & Zucc.) Benth.

Common names Kudzu vine, Kudsu.
Order Fabales.
Family Leguminosae.
Origin Far East.

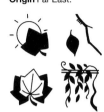

Description Very fast-growing perennial plant with woody, twining stems; in countries of origin they may grow to 100 feet (30 m). Thick, spindle-shaped, fleshy tubers up to 10 feet (3 m) long. Leaves made up of 3 large ovate segments, the lateral ones subsessile, the middle ones long-stalked. Small, papilionaceous, scented flowers, violet with a pale central spot, in long, drooping racemes. Straight, elongated, hairy fruit (legume) containing numerous brown, black-marked seeds.
Flowering period Late summer.
Cultivation Half-hardy plant to be grown outside but in regions with cold winters needs mulching round the base. Often grown as an annual in temperate climates. Sunny but sheltered position, in cool, well-drained, manured soil. Water frequently.
Propagation By seed in spring.
Use Quickly covers large surfaces. It is not recommended for cultivation in some countries, such as the United States, where it has become very invasive. In original countries the plant is grown to consolidate areas prone to landslips and as fodder. A kind of starch is extracted from the tubers and a fibrous textile from the stems.

57 RHYNCHOSIA PHASEOLOIDES DC.

Order Fabales.
Family Fabaceae.
Origin Tropical regions of America.

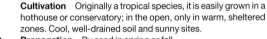
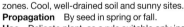
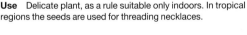

Description Perennial herbaceous plant, sometimes woody at the base. Deciduous leaves composed of 3 ovate segments, slightly pubescent below, often punctuated by red or black glands. Small papilionaceous yellow-red flowers, usually with thick down, in fairly dense racemes. Small, elongated, compressed, hairy fruit (legume) with black seeds.
Flowering period Summer.
Cultivation Originally a tropical species, it is easily grown in a hothouse or conservatory; in the open, only in warm, sheltered zones. Cool, well-drained soil and sunny sites.
Propagation By seed in spring or fall.
Use Delicate plant, as a rule suitable only indoors. In tropical regions the seeds are used for threading necklaces.

Common name Jade vine.
Order Fabales.
Family Leguminosae.
Origin Philippines.

Description   Fast-growing plant with woody stems that in natural surroundings twine themselves around trees. Large, persistent, coriaceous, shiny leaves consisting of 3 oval segments. Very big papilionaceous green flowers, up to 4 inches (10 cm), in drooping racemes up to 3 feet (1 m), pollinated by pipistrelles. The keel is large and curved, the vexillum is turned backward. Subglobose fruits with 8–10 large seeds.

Flowering period   Winter.

Cultivation   Tropical plant that requires temperatures of around 68°F (20°C) and high humidity. Rich, cool soil, not waterlogged, in fairly sunny site. Needs support.

Propagation   By cuttings in summer or by seed which, however, has a limited life (ten days or so).

Use   Delicate hothouse plant, difficult to grow but with very beautiful flowers.

Order Fabales.
Family Leguminosae.
Origin Southern Europe.

Description   Annual herbaceous plant with twining stems. Pinnate leaves with 4–5 pairs of segments, mucronate at the tip, terminating in branched tendrils. Papilionaceous, almost sessile, flowers in sparse glomerules; yellowish corolla with characteristic dark tip. Small, shortish fruit (legume) with few seeds.

Flowering period   Spring.

Cultivation   Grows well in Mediterranean and central European climates. Light-textured, well-drained soil, in sunny position. Water more frequently during early development. Needs support.

Propagation   By seed in fall or spring.

Use   Suitable for patios. It is a rather delicate and thus not a good cover plant; mainly interesting for the unusual color of its flowers.

60

WISTERIA FLORIBUNDA (Willd.) DC.

Common name
Japanese wisteria.
Order Fabales.
Family Leguminosae.
Origin Japan.

Description Vigorous, fast-growing, branching shrub with twining stems that twine clockwise. Deciduous, alternate, imparipinnate leaves with 13–19 ovate-lanceolate leaflets that are shed early in fall. Slightly scented, papilionaceous, violet-pink, 1 inch (2 cm) flowers, continuously in long, drooping racemes. Elongated, velvety-pubescent fruit (legume).

Flowering period Spring-early summer; abundant, on last year's branches.

Cultivation Hardy plant, suitable for temperate climates, even cold winters, since it tolerates frost. Sunny or partly shaded positions, in cool, rich, well-drained, preferably non-calcareous soil. Water when planting. Needs support in early stages. Prune in late winter or after flowering.

Propagation By semiripe or root cuttings in summer; by layering in late spring; also by seed in spring but growth is slower.

Varieties 'Macrobotrys,' with racemes up to 3 feet (1 m); 'Alba,' white flowers; 'Rosea,' pink flowers; 'Violaceo-Plena,' double violet flowers in looser racemes; 'Variegata,' for streaked leaves; and others.

Use Hardy and easy to cultivate (in nature it lives at greater heights than *W. sinensis*). Needs space because the roots spread. Excellent for walls and pergolas.

61

WISTERIA SINENSIS (J. Sims) Sweet
W. chinensis DC.

Common name Chinese wisteria.
Order Fabales.
Family Leguminosae.
Origin China.

Description Woody-stemmed, many-branched plant, twisting in anticlockwise direction. Deciduous, alternate, imparipinnate leaves with 9–13 ovate-lanceolate leaflets. Large papilionaceous violet flowers in long, drooping racemes; they appear before the leaves and all open at the same time on the raceme. Elongated brown-green fruit (legume), fairly narrow, broader at top, covered with fine velvety down.

Flowering period Freely in spring, with a second, less plentiful, and less scented crop in fall.

Cultivation Hardy plant, adapting well to temperate climates with harsh winters. Cool, well-drained, fairly rich soil, in sunny positions, but half-shade where the climate is warmer. Water liberally when planting. Prune after flowering to prevent branches spreading, and in late winter to encourage flowering branches to appear.

Propagation By semiripe cuttings in summer; by layering in late spring, or by seed in spring, although this produces fewer flowers.

Varieties 'Alba,' white flowers; 'Black Dragon,' double dark violet flowers that appear later, in early summer; 'Prolific,' violet, with more compact racemes, and an abundant secondary flowering period.

Use Easy to grow, this is the best-known of garden wisterias. It flowers earlier and loses leaves later than *W. floribunda*.

62

METROSIDEROS CARMINEUS W. Oliver
M. diffusus Hook

Order Myrtales.
Family Myrtaceae.
Origin New Zealand.

Description Woody, lianoid shrub with clinging roots that in natural surroundings wrap themselves around trees. Persistent, opposite, cuneate, almost sessile leaves. Small crimson flowers in large terminal inflorescences; numerous stiff, protruding stamens, deep red with yellow anthers.

Flowering period Spring.

Cultivation Does well outside in Mediterranean climates. Loose, rather dry and fairly rich soil.

Propagation By cuttings in spring.

Use Half-hardy plant that also grows well in pots. The genus is tropical, concentrated in the Pacific region, and contains many species, of which this is the hardiest.

63

QUISQUALIS INDICA L.

Common name Rangoon creeper.
Order Myrtales.
Family Combretaceae.
Origin Tropical regions of Asia.

Description Fast-growing shrub with thin, thorny stems. Semievergreen, opposite, ovate, pruinose, short-stalked leaves with yellowish veining. The stem stops growing when about 24 inches (60 cm) long and from its base new turions appear, while the main stem dies. Scented pentameral flowers with a corolla that is first white, then pink, and finally red, in compound terminal inflorescences; very long calyx, similar to a flower peduncle. Oblong, coriaceous, large, monospermous fruit.

Flowering period Summer.

Cultivation This tropical plant of warm-humid latitudes does well in the open where the temperature stays at about 50°F (10°C), otherwise in a temperate greenhouse. Sheltered and fairly sunny positions, in rich, cool soil, not waterlogged. Water plentifully before and while flowering. Needs a support.

Propagation By seed (though the plant does not always produce them in temperate zones) in spring; by young shoot cuttings in summer.

Use Delicate, but interesting for its rich, continuous flower production.

Common names
Bittersweet staff tree,
American bittersweet.
Order Celastrales.
Family Celastraceae.
Origin Northeast
America.

Description Vigorous, fast-growing shrub with twining stems. Deciduous, alternate, ovate-oblong, acuminate leaves with finely dentate margins. Small unisexual flowers (dioecious plant), greenish yellow, stellate, in large racemes or terminal panicles. The 3-valved orange-yellow fruit (capsule) opens when ripe to release the seeds, surrounded by a red aril; it appears in fall and remains for some time on the plant.

Flowering period Late spring-summer.

Cultivation Hardy plant that grows outdoors even in temperate-cold climates. Fairly undemanding as to soil and site, it does better in moist soil. Tolerates air pollution. Needs a support.

Propagation By seed in spring or fall; also by semiripe cuttings in summer.

Use Suitable for covering walls, pergolas, and trunks. To obtain fruit it is necessary to have male and female plants. It can be invasive, however, and often twines around other plants and suffocates them. As beautiful as the plant can be, it is also considered a scourge in some places.

Common name Crimson
glory vine.
Order Rhamnales.
Family Vitaceae.
Origin Japan.

Description Vigorous woody plant that climbs by tendrils. Very big, ovate-cordate deciduous leaves, slightly lobate or 3-lobed, raggedly dentate at margins, rough-haired below. In fall it takes on a reddish or reddish yellow color. Small greenish flowers, in panicles, followed by bluish fruits (berries).

Flowering period Late spring.

Cultivation Hardy species, particularly frost-resistant. Fertile, well-drained, preferably clay soil, in sunny or half-shaded positions. Water freely at first.

Propagation By cuttings or by layering in fall.

Use Highly decorative for its large red leaves in fall. Especially suitable for covering pergolas.

Common names River-bank grape, Frost grape.
Order Rhamnales.
Family Vitaceae.
Origin North America, along rivers and streams.

Description   Vigorous woody plant with lianoid stems. Deciduous, palmate-cordate leaves, usually 3-lobed, with pointed sinuses and triangular-toothed margins, shiny on both sides. Very small, scented, greenish flowers in panicles that are initially compact, then looser. Bluish black, pruinose, pea-sized, edible fruit (berry).

Flowering period   Spring.

Cultivation   Very hardy plant that adapts well outdoors even in cold winters. It also does well in shade. Cool, deep, fertile, even slightly calcareous soil.

Propagation   By cuttings, a procedure guaranteed to be successful.

Use   Widespread as rootstock because of its high resistance to phylloxera.

Common name Wine grape, European grape.
Order Rhamnales.
Family Vitaceae.
Origin Temperate parts of Europe and Asia.

Description   Woody plant with branching tendrils; the bark flakes off in long strips (unlike the *Parthenocissus* species). The leaves are deciduous, alternate, long-stalked, opposed to a tendril or inflorescence, palmate-cordate in 3–5 lobes, with dentate margins, pubescent on underside. Small, scented, greenish leaves in dense panicles; cup-shaped corolla, deciduous while flowering. Pruinose fruit (berry), yellowish, red or violet-blue, containing 1–2 seeds (pips). The wild form (*sylvestris* spp.) has unisexual flowers (dioecious plant) and violet-blue fruits that contain 3 seeds.

Flowering period   Late spring-summer.

Cultivation   Hardy or half-hardy climber, depending on cultivar. Sunny or half-shady positions, in well-drained, preferably calcareous, and fertile soil. Water frequently during periods of drought. In drier climates it is essential to irrigate in summer. Supports necessary. Prune stems to 12 inches (30 cm) from ground.

Propagation   By cuttings.

Varieties   There are thousands of cultivars, selected over many centuries. 'Purpurea,' violet-red leaves, 'Incana,' leaves pubescent white on underside.

Use   This species is most commonly used for its fruit and for making wine, but also traditionally for decorating pergolas.

68

CISSUS DISCOLOR Blume

Common name Rex-begonia vine.
Order Rhamnales.
Family Vitaceae.
Origin Java.

Description Perennial herbaceous plant, partially woody (lianoid shrub in original regions), with slender young reddish stems and branching tendrils. Large, persistent, ovate-oblong leaves with red veining, acuminate, cordate, green with silver bands above, purple below. Small greenish flowers in stalked, dense axillary racemes. Spherical black fruit (berry).
Flowering period Spring.
Cultivation Delicate plant which requires temperatures of at least 65°F (18°C). Originating in tropical rainforests, in temperate climes it grows only in the greenhouse or indoors with a high level of atmospheric humidity. Well-drained, light, rich soil, in fairly sunny or shaded sites, especially in summer. Water regularly, more sparsely in winter. Needs staking.
Propagation By semiripe cuttings in summer.
Use Difficult to grow indoors because of dry air. It can be used as a drooping subject as well as a climber. Loses many leaves in winter if the temperature is too low or if the soil is flooded.

69

CISSUS ANTARCTICA Vent.

Common name Kangaroo vine.
Order Rhamnales.
Family Vitaceae.
Origin Eastern Australia.

Description Fast-growing perennial herbaceous plant with partially woody stem (lianoid shrub in original regions) with reddish hairs. The old shoots develop tendrils. Large, persistent, ovate, acuminate leaves, roughly dentate, shiny, slightly cordate, with reddish-haired stalks. Very small greenish flowers in sparse, long-stalked axillary racemes. Spherical black fruit (berry).
Flowering period Summer.
Cultivation Half-hardy plant which grows well indoors, if not too hot, although it can tolerate a fairly dry atmosphere. Partially shady or bright position, but sheltered from direct sun, in well-drained soil.
Propagation By cuttings in summer.
Use Easy to grow, it can be kept in pots or as a drooping subject, or even raised by hydroculture. Does well in towns and cities.

70 PARTHENOCISSUS QUINQUEFOLIA (L.) Planch.

Ampelopsis quinquefolia (L.) Michx.

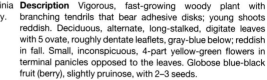

Common names Virginia creeper, Five-leafed ivy.
Order Rhamnales.
Family Vitaceae.
Origin Northeast America.

Description Vigorous, fast-growing woody plant with branching tendrils that bear adhesive disks; young shoots reddish. Deciduous, alternate, long-stalked, digitate leaves with 5 ovate, roughly dentate leaflets, gray-blue below; reddish in fall. Small, inconspicuous, 4-part yellow-green flowers in terminal panicles opposed to the leaves. Globose blue-black fruit (berry), slightly pruinose, with 2–3 seeds.

Flowering period Early summer.

Cultivation Hardy plant which does well outdoors in temperate climes. Undemanding, although it prefers rich, light, well-drained soil. It should be pruned drastically to prevent branches spreading and to encourage new growth.

Propagation Generally by hardwood cuttings in August, under glass; also by grafting.

Varieties 'Engelmannii,' smaller and narrower leaves; 'Muralis,' deeply incised leaves; 'Hirsuta,' pubescent leaves.

Use Widely used to cover large, even smooth, wall surfaces; extremely decorative, even on old trees. Hardier than *P. tricuspidata*. In wet climates it tends to run wild, growing among plants in wasteland.

71 PARTHENOCISSUS TRICUSPIDATA Planch.

Ampelopsis veitchii Siebold & Zucc.

Common name Boston ivy.
Order Rhamnales.
Family Vitaceae.
Origin Japan, China, Korea.

Description Vigorous, fast-growing woody shrub with graceful, branching stems and tendrils with adhesive disks. Highly variable, deciduous leaves, initially composed of 3 leaflets, then tautiful effect.

Flowering period Summer.

Cultivation Hardy plant which can withstand cold winters. Not too demanding as to soil and position, but does better in half-shade. Thin out in summer. Set outside from March to November, preferably with balls of soil because it will not stand transplanting with bare roots.

Propagation By semiripe cuttings in August; also by seed in late fall.

Varieties 'Lowii,' small leaves, with 3-7 wrinkled leaflets when young; 'Veitchii,' purple-flushed young leaves; and others.

Use Widely used to cover entire walls of houses and other broad surfaces.

72

AMPELOPSIS BREVIPEDUNCULATA Maxim.
A. heterophylla var. amurensis Planch.

Order Rhamnales.
Family Vitaceae.
Origin Eastern Asia.

Description Vigorous, fast-growing shrub with long, graceful, twining stems and axillary tendrils, without adhesive disks. Large, deciduous, alternate leaves that are very variable (similar to those of *Humulus* but darker), palmate, with 3–5 lobes, the lateral lobes pointed, broadly ovate-cordate, pubescent on upper side. Small greenish flowers with indistinct sepals and 4 deciduous petals, in pubescent inflorescences. Blue-violet fruit (berry) in fall, persisting for entire winter.
Flowering period Summer.
Cultivation Hardy plant but sensitive to hard frost. Cool and fairly rich soil is best. Sunny and sheltered, or shady, site. Water freely during growth phase.
Propagation By semiripe cuttings in August; also by seed.**Varieties** 'Elegans,' leaves streaked white, pink when young, rather sensitive to frost; 'Maximowiczii,' more variable leaves, also lacking lobes, without pubescence; 'Citrulloides,' leaves with 5 deep lobes, in their turn often lobate.
Use Good carpet subject for gardens and for festooning pergolas, but unsuitable for pots. Very ornamental and decorative, also for its fruits.

73

STIGMAPHYLLON CILIATUM (Lam.) Juss.

Common name Brazilian golden vine, Orchid vine, Butterfly vine, Amazon vine, Golden creeper.
Order Polygalales.
Family Malpighiaceae.
Origin Brazil.

Description Fast-growing woody plant with thin, twining stems. Persistent, opposite, acuminate leaves, hairy at margins, deeply cordate, with oblique base, the basal lobes sometimes overlapping. Large yellow flowers, the petal margins fringed, in sparse umbels; very characteristic stigmas, laminate in appearance, folded above the stamens. Small fruit (samara), surrounded by a large wing.
Flowering period Summer.
Cultivation Delicate species which needs minimum temperatures of around 65°F (18°C) and in temperate climates must be grown indoors or in a greenhouse; only in certain warm and sheltered areas can it be raised outdoors. Fertile, well-drained soil, in fairly sunny position, especially in summer, but essentially bright and sheltered. Water more plentifully during early growth and in summer. Needs support.
Propagation By semiripe cuttings in summer.
Use Unsuitable for pots.

74

CARDIOSPERMUM HALICACABUM L.

Common name Balloon vine.
Order Sapindales.
Family Sapindaceae.
Origin Tropical regions.

Description Perennial or annual plant, usually herbaceous, with branching stems and tendrils. Biternate leaves with slender ovate or lanceolate leaflets, their margins roughly and irregularly dentate. Small white flowers in sparse racemes, supported by 2 tendrils deriving from the transformation of flower buds. Subglobose, swollen, hairy, trigonal fruit (capsule), initially green, then pale and papery, containing 1-3 black seeds with a light heart-shaped mark (hence the generic name).
Flowering period Summer.
Cultivation In temperate climates it is cultivated as an annual because it does not tolerate temperatures below 41°F (5°C). Cool, well-drained soil, in fairly sunny position, sheltered from wind.
Propagation By seed in spring; the seeds retain their germinative capacity for many years.
Use Easy to cultivate, fast-growing, but not a good cover plant. The very hard seeds are used in some countries of origin for jewelry and the leaves as vegetables.

75

RHUS RADICANS L.

Common name Poison ivy.
Order Sapindales.
Family Anacardiaceae.
Origin North America.

Description Climbing shrub with clinging roots. Deciduous, ovate-rhomboid, ternate leaves, entire or slightly dentate, pubescent on underside, beautiful orange-red in fall. Small greenish flowers in panicles. Yellowish-white fruit (drupe).
Flowering period Summer.
Cultivation Hardy plant which tolerates intense cold. Sunny position, in well-drained soil.
Propagation By semiripe cuttings in summer.
Use This plant needs very careful handling by gardeners because contact with its hairs can cause allergic reactions and sometimes, as its common name suggests, serious symptoms of poisoning. In some countries, including the United States, it is not recommended to gardeners because it is considered a scourge.

76

TROPAEOLUM SPECIOSUM Poepp. & Endl.

Common names Flame nasturtium, Flame creeper.
Order Geraniales.
Family Tropaeolaceae.
Origin Southern Chile.

Description Vigorous, perennial herbaceous plant with slender stems and a somewhat fleshy rhizome. Deciduous, long-stalked, slightly fleshy leaves, smooth at margins, pruinose, initially reddish, then blue-green, digitate with 6 short-stalked, obovate leaflets. The solitary, long-stalked, axillary flowers at the tips of the branches are bright red, with a long, fairly straight spur; the apical petals are bilobate, the 2 upper petals being smaller and the 3 lower ones narrowing into a claw, with a yellow limb at the base. Subglobose, violet-blue fruit (schizocarp).
Flowering period Summer.
Cultivation Hardy plant which adapts well to cold climates provided the base is mulched with dry leaves in winter. Cool, well-drained, rich, preferably lime-free soil. Water frequently because it hates drought. Plenty of fertilizer helps to develop the leaves, not the flowers. Sunny position but lower part must always be kept in shade. Needs support.
Propagation By seed in spring; by rhizome cuttings at end of winter.
Use Does well and is easy to grow in pots. It is the strongest and most spectacular of all the *Tropaeolum* species.

77

TROPAEOLUM TRICOLORUM Sweet

Order Geraniales.
Family Tropaeolaceae.
Origin Chile.

Description Perennial herbaceous plant with slender stems and small tubers. Deciduous leaves with 5–7 ovate-linear lobes. Small flowers of various colors: calyx blue, violet, yellow or orange-red with black tip; corolla yellow-orange with 5 petals, the 2 upper ones spatulate, the 3 lower ones with a smaller limb, narrowing toward the base; spur red to yellow, straight or sometimes curved. The fruit (schizocarp) divides into 3 mericarps at maturity.
Flowering period Spring-summer.
Cultivation Half-hardy plant, often cultivated as an annual in cold climates. Well-drained, loose, lime-free soil, in sunny position. Water freely during early growth, more sparingly during dormant period. Plentiful fertilization stimulates photosythesis and also flowering.
Propagation By seed in spring; by tuber cuttings in winter.
Use Easy to grow, it also does well in pots.

78

HEDERA CANARIENSIS Willd.

Common names Canary Island ivy, Algerian ivy, Madeira ivy.
Order Apiales.
Family Araliaceae.
Origin Canaries and northwest Africa.

Description Fast-growing shrub with clinging roots and reddish stems. Persistent, alternate, shiny, coriaceous, soft leaves, turning bronze in winter, cordate, ovate-triangular, those of the sterile branches 3–5 lobed, those of the fertile branches almost entire and smaller; wine-red stalks. Small, yellowish-green flowers in umbels; no calyx. Black fruit (berry).
Flowering period Late summer.
Cultivation Half-hardy plant which survives cold winters if grown in sheltered position, either sunny or shady. Cool, well-drained soil in sites that are not too dry.
Propagation By cuttings in spring or summer.
Varieties 'Souvenir de Marengo,' leaves streaked gray, with creamy white margins; 'Ravensholst,' large leaves, strongest of all; 'Azorica,' slightly lobate, downy brown leaves.
Use Can also be grown in pots; very suitable for indoors.

79

HEDERA COLCHICA Koch

Common names Persian ivy, Fragrant ivy, Colchis ivy.
Order Apiales.
Family Araliaceae.
Origin Caucasus and northern Iran.

Description Fast-growing shrub with clinging roots. Shoots bear yellowish down. The persistent leaves are large, alternate, ovate-elliptical, acuminate, cordate, soft, entire or slightly lobate, dull green above and yellowish green below; those of fertile branches are smaller. Small yellow-green flowers in umbels; distinct calyx. Black fruit (berry).
Flowering period Late summer.
Cultivation Hardy species which does well outside in temperate climes; not very demanding, it needs cool, deep soil. Water freely during early growth.
Propagation Especially by cuttings in spring or summer.
Varieties The variegated cultivars are less hardy and do not tolerate direct sunlight. 'Sulphur Heart,' yellow-centered leaves; 'Dentata,' large, drooping leaves with slightly dentate margins; 'Dentata Variegata,' pale-edged, gray-centered leaves; and others.
Use Very beautiful, suitable as a carpeting subject. Also does well in pots.

80

HEDERA HELIX L.

Common names
Common ivy, English ivy.
Order Apiales.
Family Araliaceae.
Origin Europe.

Description   Climbing plant with stems that produce, on the side facing the support, an abundance of clinging roots. Older specimens may be as large as trees. Fairly slow growth rate at start. Persistent, alternate, coriaceous, soft, long-stalked shiny leaves, of two types: those of the nonflowering branches are 3–5 lobed, those of the flowering branches ovate, acuminate, entire and bigger. Small yellowish green flowers in umbels of 8–20, in turn grouped 2–3 to the tips of the branches; calyx absent, petals turned backward. The dull black fruit (berry) is poisonous, like the whole plant, and matures the following spring.

Flowering period   End summer-fall; on higher branches.

Cultivation   Hardy species which in the open withstands cold winters. Undemanding in respect of exposure or soil. Cool, shady (even north-facing) positions, in rich, well-drained, slightly alkaline soil. Prune in spring. The cultivars with variegated or yellowish leaves are less hardy and prefer brighter positions.

Propagation   Especially by cuttings in spring or late summer; also by seed and layering.

Varieties   There are hundreds of cultivars that differ in the color and shape of leaves, in hardiness and in size. 'Eva,' blue-green leaves, whitish near margins; 'Pedata,' leaves with straight segments, the middle one very long; 'Lobata,' pronounced leaf lobes; 'Atropurpurea,' leaves turning violet in winter.

Use   The species is easy to cultivate and is suitable for pots. It tolerates atmospheric pollution. The plant can be grown indoors, if the temperature is not too hot. Potentially a weed, it often grows wild in woodland.

Above: inflorescence formed of an umbel of black berries, enjoyed by birds, the principal disseminators of the species. Opposite: the conspicuous late-summer flowers.

81 ALLAMANDA CATHARTICA L.

Common names
Common allamanda,
Golden trumpet.
Order Gentianales.
Family Apocynaceae.
Origin Tropical South
America.

Description   Fast-growing, rambling perennial shrub. Persistent, sessile leaves, in whorls of 3–4, entire, coriaceous, lanceolate and shiny. Large, showy, funnel-shaped, violet-yellow flowers, with a flat limb divided into 5 lobes, in terminal, axillary racemes. Elongated fruit (follicle), with feathery seeds.
Flowering period   From July until first frosts.
Cultivation   The plant can be grown in the greenhouse, conservatory or indoors. It survives in the open only in warm, sheltered sites where the temperature does not fall below 54°F (12°C). It prefers bright positions but not in direct sunlight, and rich, well-aerated soil. Water regularly, but less often in winter. At the end of winter, prune the branches above the second node and manure thoroughly; the plant will then develop rapidly. During growth it is advisable to tie and bend the branches into an arc-shape; this will produce more flowers.
Propagation   By nonflowering branch cuttings in spring.
Varieties   'Grandiflora,' wholly yellow flowers; 'Williamsii,' yellow flowers with pink fauces (this is the cultivar most resistant to cold and better suited to growing in a pot because it does not spread too much); 'Schiottii,' yellow flowers with brown-streaked fauces; 'Hendersonii,' yellow-orange flowers.
Use   Better indoors than outdoors in temperate climates. In addition to being allowed to climb, the plant can also be kept as a shrub, with frequent pruning of branches, or grown in large pots.

82 BEAUMONTIA GRANDIFLORA (Roxb.) Wall.

Common name Herald's
trumpet.
Order Gentianales.
Family Apocynaceae.
Origin Northern India.

Description   Shrub with paired stems, reddish when young. Large, persistent, opposite, ovate-oblong leaves, shiny above, velvety below, acuminate, with undulate margin. Highly scented, showy white flowers, 6–8 to the terminal corymb; funnel-shaped, 5-lobed corolla with undulate margin. Long, narrow fruit (follicle) which opens halfway but stays joined at both ends.
Flowering period   Late spring-summer, on previous year's branches.
Cultivation   Half-hardy plant which needs dry and fairly warm winters, 45°–50°F (7°–10°C) and warm, humid summers. Light, well-drained, fertile soil, in bright position. Water frequently during growth and in summer. Needs support. Prune after flowering.
Propagation   By semiripe cuttings in summer, but rooting is difficult; by seed, but does not produce fruit in temperate climates.
Variety   'Superba,' larger leaves.
Use   In temperate climes it grows well on patios and in conservatories, but not in pots. Very suitable for festoons. In India the bark is used for making a fibrous textile.

83

MANDEVILLA SANDERI (Hemsl.) Woodson
Dipladenia sanderi Hemsl.

Order Gentianales.
Family Apocynaceae.
Origin Brazil.

Description Shrub with twining stems. Deciduous, opposite, coriaceous, shiny, oblong leaves. Large unscented flowers, 3-5 to the axillary raceme, pink with yellow fauces, paler as they fade.
Flowering period Late summer, continuously.
Cultivation Delicate species which requires a minimum temperature of 60°F (15°C) and a bright position. Water frequently, more sparingly in winter. Trim regularly to stimulate new shoots. Needs staking. Liable to attack by red spider mite.
Propagation By hardwood cuttings in late winter or by semiripe cuttings in late summer.
Variety 'Brazilian Jasmine,' smaller leaves and pink flowers.
Use Grown mainly indoors or in the conservatory.

84

MANDEVILLA LAXA (Ruiz & Pav.) Woodson
Mandevilla suavolens Lindl.

Common name Chilean jasmine.
Order Gentianales.
Family Apocynaceae.
Origin Argentina and Bolivia.

Description Climbing plant, initially slow- and then fast-growing, with twining stems. Deciduous or semievergreen leaves, opposite, ovate-cordate, short-stalked, shiny, acuminate. Large, scented, funnel-shaped, 5-lobed white flowers, in axillary racemes at tips of branches.
Flowering period Continuously, in summer.
Cultivation Half-hardy plant which can live outside with temperatures under 50°F (10°C). If grown outdoors, mulch the base with dry leaves and straw before winter arrives, and keep sheltered. Rich, well-drained soil, not waterlogged. Water frequently during early growth, more sparingly later. Prune branches after flowering. Grow in half-shade, especially in summer, as direct sunlight stains the leaves brown and can encourage attacks of red spider mite.
Propagation By semiripe cuttings in summer; by seed in fall or late winter.
Use Grow in open ground or, better still, in large pots that can be taken inside in winter. If the climate is temperate, the stem often sheds leaves at the base. It is interesting for its lovely flowers, but provides little cover.

TRACHELOSPERMUM JASMINOIDES
Lem.

Common name Star jasmine.
Order Gentianales.
Family Apocynaceae.
Origin China.

Description   Vigorous shrub, fast-growing only in early years, with twining stems and clinging roots. Persistent, opposite, coriaceous, shiny, ovate-oblong leaves, pubescent on underside when young. Small, highly scented white flowers, tending to turn creamy when they fade, in long-stalked, mostly terminal, axillary corymbs; flat corolla with a short tube and limb of 5 trapezoidal lobes, all slanting on the same side. Bivalve, elongated fruit (follicle) with crested seeds.

Flowering period   Continuously and freely in summer.

Cultivation   Half-hardy climber that does not tolerate frost. In temperate climates with cold winters it needs to be planted against a wall and mulched in winter with dry leaves and straw. Undemanding as to exposure, but sunny positions encourage more flowers. Water regularly, more often in summer, including the leaves if the plant is in full sun. Rich, well-drained soil, not waterlogged.

Propagation   By semiripe cuttings in fall; by seed in spring; by layering in summer.

Varieties   'Angustifolium,' small, narrow leaves; 'Variegatum,' streaked leaves with irregular margins; 'Wilsonii,' narrower leaves, reddish in winter.

Use   Easy to cultivate, very suitable for balconies and patios. Much used in Mediterranean region for climbing and partial carpeting.

Common name Cruel plant
Order Gentianales.
Family Asclepiadaceae.
Origin Southern regions of South America.

Description Fast-growing woody plant with latex-filled stems that often twine in pairs. Persistent, ovate-oblong, short-stalked, paired leaves, downy on underside. The axillary white flowers of 1¼ inches (3 cm), in large inflorescences, are made up of 5 large sepals and a tubular 5-lobed corolla. The flowers are visited by pollinating insects, usually at night by moths, which remain trapped until the following morning but are not killed (despite the plant's common name). The large pear-shaped fruit (follicle) contains numerous flattened, blackish seeds furnished with long, silky hairs.

Flowering period Midsummer-early fall. The flowers appear continuously for about a month.

Cultivation The plant, from tropical and subtropical zones, only does well outside in temperate climates if the site is sheltered, close to walls; it is better grown in pots, brought inside for the winter, in the conservatory or in the greenhouse. A sunny position encourages flower growth. Loose, humus-rich, well-drained soil.

Propagation In warm surroundings, by seed in spring or by hardwood cuttings in late summer.

Use Half-hardy plant which is suitable for covering broad surfaces quickly. It can be cultivated as an annual by sowing seed in February under glass and moving outside in May.

Common names Wax plant, Honey plant.
Order Gentianales.
Family Asclepiadaceae.
Origin Southern China and North Australia.

Description Vigorous perennial herbaceous plant with graceful stems and clinging roots. Leaves persistent, opposite, fleshy, ovate-oblong, pointed, short-stalked, shiny, and coriaceous. Small, generally scented, flowers in compact, drooping, spherical, axillary umbels; rotate corolla with 5 fleshy pink lobes, surmounted in the center by a corona of 5-segmented nectaries. fruit (follicle) containing seeds with long silky hairs.

Flowering period Summer.

Cultivation Delicate, half-hardy climber which can be grown in the open only where the temperature does not fall below 50°F (10°C). Bright position but not direct sunlight, which turns leaves yellow. Water regularly but much less in winter. Rich, light, well-drained soil. Needs staking. Do not remove the flower peduncles which produce new flowers the following year.

Propagation By semiripe cuttings in summer, flowering after 2–3 years; or by layering.

Varieties Cultivars require higher temperatures and produce fewer flowers. 'Variegata,' variegated leaves with reddish margins; 'Exotica,' yellow-centered leaves.

Use Easy to cultivate, best grown in pots, also by hydroculture. Does well indoors since it tolerates a dry atmosphere.

Common names
Umbrella flower,
Parachute plant.
Order Gentianales.
Family Asclepiadaceae.
Origin South Africa
(Natal).

Description Succulent shrub with twining, reddish stems. Small semievergreen leaves, ovate-triangular, opposite, acuminate-mucronate and succulent, especially those at the tips of young branches. The large, strangely shaped flowers, light green with dark spots, appear in small groups, facing upward; the corolla, swollen at the base, continues as a tube, initially narrow, then widening into a funnel, and divided at the tip into 5 very long lobes that converge at the top and spread out and down in a kind of "parachute."

Flowering period Summer-fall.

Cultivation Delicate species that will not tolerate temperatures lower than 50°F (10°C) but can be grown in open ground if planted against a wall in warm coastal zones. Well-drained soil, dry in winter, in fairly sunny position. Do not remove the flower peduncles, from which new flowers develop.

Propagation By seed in spring (though the cultivated form seldom produces these); by cuttings in summer.

Use Very interesting for its flowers, the plant is grown in small pots, in the hothouse or indoors. The genus *Ceropegia*, comprising some 160 species, is distributed through the tropics of the Old World. The curious flowers are pollinated by small flies which remain trapped until they have gathered all the pollen, which they then carry to other flowers.

The drawings show details of the very curious flowers of the parachute plant. Their strange form is no freak of nature but a sophisticated device for attracting pollinating insects. Right: details showing the twisted shape of the flower buds, typical of all the Gentianales.

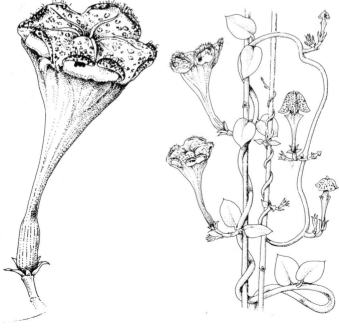

89

OXYPETALUM CAERULEUM (D. Don) Decaisne
Tweedia caerulea D. Don

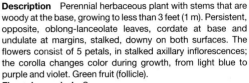

Order Gentianales.
Family Asclepiadaceae.
Origin Brazil and Uruguay.

Description Perennial herbaceous plant with stems that are woody at the base, growing to less than 3 feet (1 m). Persistent, opposite, oblong-lanceolate leaves, cordate at base and undulate at margins, stalked, downy on both surfaces. The flowers consist of 5 petals, in stalked axillary inflorescences; the corolla changes color during growth, from light blue to purple and violet. Green fruit (follicle).

Flowering period Summer.

Cultivation Half-hardy plant that lives outside in coastal zones with warm winters, often grown as an annual. Sunny position, in rich, well-drained clay soil. Water freely in summer, less in winter. Needs support. Prune tips to encourage side shoots.

Propagation By seed in spring; by cuttings in spring, under glass, when it roots easily.

Use Not a good cover plant but interesting for its showy flowers. Suitable for growing in pots on well-exposed patios and balconies.

The drawing shows a detail of the plant and the opposite leaves, characteristic of the Asclepiadaceae.

90

PERIPLOCA GRAECA L.

Common name Silk vine.
Order Gentianales.
Family Asclepiadaceae.
Origin Eastern
Mediterranean area.

Description Very fast-growing, vigorous, perennial herbaceous plant with thin, twining stems. The deciduous, opposite, shiny, ovate-elliptical leaves remain for some while on the plant in fall. The small flowers are yellowish green on the outside, brown-violet inside, with 5 spreading or backward-turning, hairy lobes; they bloom plentifully in long-stalked axillary inflorescences. The paired fruits (follicles) are joined at the tips and contain seeds with silky hairs.
Flowering period Summer.
Cultivation Hardy plant that needs well-drained, preferably cool and deep soil, in a sunny position.
Propagation By seed in spring; by semiripe cuttings in summer.
Use Still found growing wild in some coastal woods of the Mediterranean zone, but likely to become extinct as its habitat becomes built up. Very suitable for pergolas in sites close to the sea. Potentially a weed that tends to twine around other plants and suffocate them, it should be pruned regularly to ensure its containment.

91

STEPHANOTIS FLORIBUNDA Brongn.

Common names
Madagascar jasmine,
Floradora.
Order Gentianales.
Family Asclepiadaceae.
Origin Madagascar.

Description Slow-growing, none too vigorous shrub with thin stems. Leaves persistent, opposite, ovate-oblong, short-stalked, coriaceous, sometimes mucronate, and shiny. Highly scented white flowers in dense axillary umbels; small 5-lobed calyx and long coralline tube that expands into 5 large, spreading lobes. Long fruit (follicle) containing seeds with silky hairs.
Flowering period Late spring-summer; freely and continuously on branches of the year.
Cultivation Delicate climber which in temperate climes is suitable for verandas and conservatories; winter temperatures should be kept at around 57°F (14°C). Rich, well-drained soil, in bright positions, but with no direct sun in summer. Water regularly, less in winter. Shorten tips in late winter. Needs staking. Often infested by scale insects.
Propagation By cuttings in spring or summer; by seed in spring.
Variety 'Elvaston,' more flowers and denser umbels.
Use Particularly suitable for growing in pots. Withstands a dry indoor atmosphere, providing the leaves are sprayed, better than other tropical species. Not good for cover.

92 SALPICHROA ORIGANIFOLIA (Lam.) Baill.
S. rhomboidea (Gillies & Hook.) Miers

Common name Cock's-eggs.
Order Solanales.
Family Solanaceae.
Origin South America.

Description Fast-growing perennial herbaceous plant; stems woody at base and flexible at tip. Deciduous, ovate-rhomboidal, long-stalked leaves. Small, solitary, paired, long-stalked, drooping, white, 5-lobed tubular flowers. Ovoid fruit (berry). white to brownish when mature.
Flowering period Summer.
Cultivation Half-hardy plant which grows well outdoors in Mediterranean climates, where it bears mature fruit. In cooler zones it needs the protection of a wall. Sunny position, in loose, well-drained soil.
Propagation By cuttings.
Use Grows wild along hedges and in walls in parts of the Mediterranean zone.

93 SOLANDRA MAXIMA (Sessé & Moc.) P.S. Green

Common names Capa de oro, Golden chalice vine.
Order Solanales.
Family Solanaceae.
Origin Mexico.

Description Perennial climber with woody, twining stems; in regions of origin it reaches a length of 165 feet (50 m). Evergreen, stalked, ovate, coriaceous, shiny leaves. Showy, scented, solitary, funnel-shaped flowers with a long corolline tube that broadens into 5 yellow, reflex lobes, crinkly at margins. The flower opens in the evening. Globose fruit (berry).
Flowering period Spring-summer.
Cultivation The plant grows well outdoors in temperate-warm climates where the winter temperature stays at around 54°F (12°C). Sunny position, in rich, well-drained soil. Water freely during growth, rarely in winter. Excessive feeding and watering in spring and summer will impede development of flowers. Needs support.
Propagation By semiripe cuttings in summer; also by seed.
Use Easy to cultivate, it also does well in pots.

Common name Potato vine.
Order Solanales.
Family Solanaceae.
Origin Brazil.

Description Branching shrub with thin stems, climbing by means of leaf stalks. The evergreen, stalked, ovate-acuminate leaves are variable in form (entire or divided into 2–5 lobes). Flowers with 5 stellate blue petals in dense terminal racemes.
Flowering period Summer to fall, on branches of the year.
Cultivation Half-hardy plant which needs minimum temperatures of around 46°–47°F (7°–8°C) but also survives colder winters if grown against a wall and mulched at the base with dry leaves. Sunny, sheltered positions, in rich, well-drained soil. Water freely during growth, more sparingly in winter. Shorten tips in late winter. Needs support.
Propagation By cuttings in late summer; by seed in spring.
Varieties 'Album,' white flowers; 'Grandiflorum,' denser racemes; 'Floribundum,' more flowers.
Use Grows well in pots.

Common names Potato vine, Giant potato creeper, Paradise flower.
Order Solanales.
Family Solanaceae.
Origin Costa Rica.

Description Perennial plant with stems that bear scattered short, hooked thorns. Evergreen, alternate, variously shaped leaves, simple or trilobed and cordate at the top, pinnate with 4-6 pairs of leaflets lower down. The large flowers are initially violet, then blue, with a rotate corolla, appearing continuously in dense, drooping, terminal racemes.
Flowering period Summer-early fall, on branches of the year.
Cultivation The plant is more delicate than *S. jasminoides* and does well in Mediterranean zones where the temperature is always above 50°F (10°C). Fertile, cool, well-drained, even slightly calcareous soil, in sheltered but sunny positions. Water freely during growth. Needs support.
Propagation By cuttings at end of summer; also by seed in spring although rarely bears fruit in temperate climates.
Use Easy to grow and does well in pots.

96

STREPTOSOLEN JAMESONII (Benth.) Miers

Common names
Marmalade bush, Firebush, Orange browallia, Yellow heliotrope.

Order Solanales.
Family Solanaceae.
Origin Colombia, Andes.

Description Fast-growing shrub with bushy habit and branches that are pubescent at the tip. Persistent, ovate, alternate, stalked leaves, velvety on underside, pointed at the tip and base. Tubular, stalked flowers with yellow corolline tube and deep orange lobes, in dense terminal panicles.

Flowering period Spring-summer; continuously and freely.

Cultivation Half-hardy plant that requires minimum temperatures of not lower than 45°F (7°C). Sunny and very bright, but sheltered, positions, in loose, rich, even slightly alkaline soil, without puddles. Does not tolerate intense heat. Water more freely in summer. Prune lightly after flowering. Needs support.

Propagation By nonflowering branch cuttings in early spring or by semiripe cuttings in late summer.

Use The plant can easily be grown as a climber, and also in a pot. The huge family Solanaceae is important, both for edible purposes and for its large number of highly decorative species. Among the former, in addition to the potato and the tomato, are plants that are vital to the food economy in tropical countries, such as the pepino (*Solanum muricatum*), the lulo (*S. quitoense*), the cocono (*S. topiro*) and the tree tomato (*Cyphomandra betacea*). Among the latter are the innnumerable cultivars of petunias and tobacco plants, the winter cherries (*Physalis alkelengi*, *P. franchetii*), and the various splendid, gigantic trumpet flowers of the genus *Datura*.

Detail of the flowers, similar in appearance and structure to the petunias. These flowers are pollinated by butterflies and wasps.

97

CONVOLVULUS MAURITANICUS Boiss.

Order Solanales.
Family Convolvulaceae.
Origin North Africa.

Description Perennial herbaceous plant with thin, creeping, slightly twining stems covered with soft white hairs. Deciduous, alternate, ovate-elliptical, short-stalked, rounded leaves. Large, flat, funnel-shaped, axillary flowers, violet blue with white fauces, in small groups.

Flowering period Late spring; freely and continuously, sometimes with second crop in fall.

Cultivation Half-hardy plant that does not tolerate frost but does well outside in sheltered sites, even in heavy soil. Water regularly.

Propagation By seed, directly in ground outside, in spring; by cuttings in summer.

Use Easy to grow, suitable for covering walls. It can be troublesome in gardens because of its prolific growth, so should be watched for invasiveness.

98

CONVOLVULUS TRICOLOR L.

Common names Dwarf bindweed, Dwarf morning glory.
Order Solanales.
Family Convolvulaceae.
Origin Southwest Europe.

Description Fast-growing, vigorous, branching annual herbaceous plant; shrubby or climbing habit. Alternate, ovate-lanceolate, pointed leaves, with hairs at margins and along veins. Large, solitary, funnel-shaped, long-stalked flowers, at axils of upper leaves; corolla with 3 bands of color, violet-blue outside, then white, with yellow fauces. Hairy fruit (capsule).

Flowering period Freely in summer.

Cultivation Hard-hardy plant that does not tolerate frost. Grow in a sunny but sheltered position, in rich, well-drained, even alkaline soil. Needs support. Remove ripe fruits to prolong flowering.

Propagation By seed in spring, directly in ground outside.

Varieties There are numerous cultivars, including the following climbers which reach several yards in length, the natural form measuring around 16 inches (40 cm); 'Flying Saucers,' white- and blue-banded flowers; 'Heavenly Blue,' white-centered flowers and heart-shaped leaves; 'Major,' blue, red and white flowers.

Use Easy to grow, adapting well to pots. Like *Convolvulus mauritanicus* (see above) , this can be troublesome and should be watched for invasiveness.

Order Solanales.
Family Convolvulaceae.
Origin Southeast Europe.

Description Vigorous, fast-growing perennial herbaceous plant with slender, twining, angular stems. Deciduous, stalked leaves, cordate with obtuse basal lobes. Large, solitary, long-stalked, funnel-shaped white flowers; calyx concealed by 2 conspicuous ovate bracts (a distinctive feature of convolvuli). Fruit (capsule) papery when mature, containing several seeds.
Flowering period From spring to late summer.
Cultivation Hardy plant which can withstand cold winters. Undemanding as to soil but needs some coolure and good drainage. Fairly sunny positions. Water freely before flowering.
Propagation By seed in spring; by root cuttings in spring and fall.
Variety 'Incarnata,' pink flowers.
Use Easy to cultivate, in open ground and pots, it grows rapidly to cover fences and trellises. It can be invasive, so its growth should be watched.

Order Solanales.
Family Convolvulaceae.
Origin Mexico.

Description Vigorous, fast-growing perennial herbaceous plant with twining, paired, reddish stems. Deciduous, palmate-cordate leaves, divided into 3 deep lobes, the middle one narrow at the base, borne on reddish stalks. Numerous tubular flowers, red in bud, then yellow and orange, finally whitish, in unilateral, axillary racemes; protruding stamens.
Flowering period Summer, freely and continuously.
Cultivation Half-hardy plant which in cold climates is often grown as an annual. Sunny but sheltered position, as exposure to midday heat can cause leaves to turn yellow. Rich, cool, light soil, without puddles, but always damp, especially in summer. Remove faded leaves to prolong flowering.
Propagation By seed in spring, under glass in cold climates. Sensitive to transplanting.
Use Grows well outside or in pots; delicate foliage.

101

IPOMOEA QUAMOCLIT L.
Quamoclit pinnata (L.) Voigt

Common names
Cypress vine, Cardinal climber, Star-glory.
Order Solanales.
Family Convolvulaceae.
Origin Tropical regions.

Description Fast-growing perennial herbaceous plant with thin, twining stems. Persistent, sessile, ovate leaves, deeply divided into threadlike lobes. Large, long-stalked, tubular, scarlet, 5-segmented flowers, in groups of 1–3 at leaf axils.
Flowering period Late summer.
Cultivation Half hardy plant which does well outside in places sheltered from the wind. It is grown in temperate climates as an annual. Cool, well-drained, slightly fertilized soil, in sunny positions. Water freely in growth phase.
Propagation By seed in spring, best directly in ground outside; also by cuttings in summer.
Varieties 'Alba,' white flowers; 'Rosea,' pink flowers.
Use Delicate foliage; early flowers, even during first phases of growth.

102

IPOMOEA HORSFALLIAE Hook.

Order Solanales.
Family Convolvulaceae.
Origin West Indies.

Description Vigorous perennial plant with woody stems. Persistent, coriaceous, stalked leaves with 5–7 deep lobes, acuminate, with undulate margins. Large crimson flowers with a long corolla and 5 long-stalked, flat, disklike lobes, in axillary, terminal inflorescences. Seldom produces ripe seeds in temperate climes.
Flowering period Freely, in winter.
Cultivation Delicate plant that cannot tolerate intense cold. Cool, rich, even somewhat clayey soil, in sunny, warm but sheltered position.
Propagation By cuttings in summer; also by seed in late winter, under glass.
Varieties 'Alba,' white flowers; 'Lady Slade,' pale pink flowers; 'Briggsii,' larger flowers.
Use Suitable for conservatories and patios. Interesting for its winter flowers.

103   IPOMOEA HEDERACEA Jacq.
Pharbitis hederacea (Jacq.) Choisy

Common name Morning glory.
Order Solanales.
Family Convolvulaceae.
Origin Tropical regions of America.

Description Annual herbaceous plant. Large, variably shaped leaves, usually cordate-triangular with 3 lobes, the middle one pointed. Funnel-shaped, blue-violet flowers.
Flowering period Summer.
Cultivation Half-hardy plant, to be grown outside only in warmer zones. Cool, light, rich soil, in sunny but sheltered position.
Propagation By seed in spring.
Variety 'Limbata,' purple-pink flowers.
Use For covering walls, fences, and trellises. It climbs freely over tree trunks, covering them with its showy flowers.

104   IPOMOEA TRICOLOR Cav.
Ipomoea rubrocaerulea Hook. f.

Common name Morning glory.
Order Solanales.
Family Convolvulaceae.
Origin Mexico.

Description Fast-growing perennial herbaceous plant with slender, graceful, twining stems, branched at top, semiwooded at base. Semideciduous, ovate-cordate, acuminate, short-stalked leaves. Large, showy, funnel-shaped flowers, 3–4 to a pedunculate raceme; corolla white in bud, then red with white fauces; flowers remain open for a single day.
Flowering period Freely in summer.
Cultivation Half-hardy plant, often grown as an annual in temperate zones; raised as a perennial in the greenhouse. Light, rich, well-drained, slightly alkaline soil, in sunny, sheltered position. Needs support in early stages of growth. Remove faded blooms to prolong flowering period.
Propagation By seed in spring, directly outside, provided no likelihood of late frosts. The germinative power of the seeds is greater if they are soaked in warm water for 12 hours.
Varieties 'Flying Saucer,' blue and white flowers; 'Heavenly Blue' and 'Blue Star,' blue flowers; 'Alba,' white flowers.
Use Very suitable for patios because it is so easy to grow in pots; grows fast and provides rapid cover for trellises.

Common names Cup-and-saucer vine, Mexican ivy.

Order Solanales.

Family Polemoniaceae.

Origin Central and South America.

Description Plant with a woody habit in mild climates, a herbaceous perennial or annual in colder areas, branching from the base. The stems are slender when young, then stronger; climbs by means of branched tendrils. Paripinnate leaves consisting of 2–3 pairs of elliptical leaflets. Large, bell-shaped, solitary, long-stalked flowers at axes of upper leaves, initially yellow-green, then violet, with a broad calyx and 5-lobed corolla. Coriaceous fruit (capsule).

Flowering period Midsummer to fall frosts. In greenhouse, from spring to early winter.

Cultivation Can be grown in the open only where the temperature is above 39°F (4°C); it dies at the first frosts. The plant flowers more abundantly in a sunny position and when not fed too frequently. Loose, humus-rich soil, with fertilizer only during growth phase. Water freely in summer. The young branches are weak and need to be supported. Readily attacked by aphids and red spider mites.

Propagation The seeds are very fertile and, if set in a seedbed in March, will develop rapidly, producing plants that flower in the same year; also by cuttings in spring.

Varieties 'Flore albo,' greenish-white flowers; 'Variegata,' streaked flowers.

Use Half-hardy plant, easy to cultivate. It is very suitable for covering trellises and pergolas, tending to spread upward. It can also be grown in pots. Plants obtained from seed and which flower in the same year are better than old specimens for covering high fences.

The large paired flowers, initially greenish-yellow, then violet, are the most obvious characteristic of this climber. In its original countries the cup-and-saucer vine is pollinated by bats.

Common names
Bleeding-heart vine,
Bleeding glory-bower.
Order Lamiales.
Family Verbenaceae.
Origin Tropical West
Africa.

Description Vigorous plant with almost twining stems. Persistent, ovate-acuminate, opposite, short-stalked leaves. Showy flowers in dense, drooping inflorescences; corolla with 5 red petals, on a calyx of 3 whitish, lantern-shaped sepals; markedly protruding stamens. Bluish fruit (berry), enfolded in a persistent calyx.

Flowering period Summer, on branches of the year.

Cultivation Delicate plant that requires minimum temperatures of around 57°F (14°C). In temperate-warm climates the plant loses its leaves in winter. Bright positions, partially shaded in summer, and high atmospheric humidity encourage profuse flower growth. Fairly rich soil, even slightly clayey, not waterlogged. Water frequently in summer, less during winter dormancy. Needs support in early growth stages.

Propagation By herbaceous cuttings in spring or semiripe cuttings in summer; also by seed.

Varieties 'Balfouri,' large flowers; 'Variegatum,' variegated flowers.

Use Best grown in the conservatory, on the patio or indoors, with high atmospheric humidity. It also grows very freely in open ground.

Common name Queen's
wreath.
Order Lamiales.
Family Verbenaceae.
Origin Central America.

Description Woody shrub with twining stems that reaches 40 feet (12 m) in countries of origin. Persistent, opposite, coriaceous, subsessile, elliptical leaves. Short-stalked violet flowers in dense, elongated, terminal racemes; sepals longer than and alternate to petals, colored during flowering, persisting until fruit matures.

Flowering period From spring to late summer.

Cultivation Delicate plant that needs temperatures above 60°F (15°C), but can live outside in warm, sheltered zones. Tends to lose its leaves in winter. Bright but not too sunny positions in summer, in rich, well-drained, light soil. Water less frequently during dormant phase. Needs staking.

Propagation By semiripe cuttings in summer.

Variety 'Albiflora', white flowers.

Use Its dense flowers are very decorative; suitable for pots in the conservatory.

108

BUDDLEIA MADAGASCARIENSIS Lam
Nicodemia madagascariensis (Lam.)

Order Scrophulariales.
Family Buddleiaceae.
Origin Madagascar.

Description Shrub with arching branches. Large, persistent, rough, narrowly lanceolate, acuminate, shiny leaves, downy white on underside, cordate or rounded at the base. Small, fragrant flowers with a long corolline tube and 4–5 deep yellow petals, in long terminal panicles.

Flowering period Spring, on branches of the year.

Cultivation Half-hardy plant that does not tolerate cold. Plant against a wall and protect the base with dry leaves in winter. Sunny but sheltered position, in cool, rich, well-drained soil. Water freely in summer and prune drastically in late winter. Needs staking.

Propagation By semiripe cuttings in late summer; also by seed in spring.

Use Easy to grow; also does well in large pots.

109

JASMINUM HUMILE L.

Common name Yellow jasmine.
Order Scrophulariales.
Family Oleaceae.
Origin Central-eastern Asia.

Description Shrub with bare, green, rather angular branches. Semievergreen, alternate leaves, usually formed of 3–5 segments, the terminal one being slightly bigger. Erect or pendulous yellow flowers in cymes of 5–12, the corolla lobes often reflex. The fruit is an ovoid berry.

Flowering period First half of summer.

Cultivation Half-hardy plant that withstands fairly brief periods of frost. In winter it tends to lose its leaves. Light textured, well-drained, preferably calcareous soil, in full sun, sheltered from wind. Prune well after flowering.

Propagation By semiripe cuttings in late spring.

Varieties Rather variable species. Among the numerous cultivars are 'Revolutum,' with highly scented flowers, *farreri*, with evergreen leaves and a very long terminal segment, and *Wallichianum*, with cymes of 1–3 flowers.

Use For covering walls, fences, and rocks. Easy to grow, it has no particular requirements and is resistant to summer drought in warm zones.

110

JASMINUM AZORICUM L.
J. trifoliatum Moench

Order Scrophulariales.
Family Oleaceae.
Origin Madeira.

Description Vigorous shrub with thin cylindrical stems. Persistent, opposite leaves, composed of 3 ovate, coriaceous, wavy-edged leaflets, the middle larger than the others. Scented white flowers with a long corolline tube and 5 narrow lobes opening in a star, in axillary inflorescences.

Flowering period Summer, on branches of the year.

Cultivation Half-hardy plant that does not tolerate frost. In cooler climates it often partially loses its leaves in winter and needs to be brought inside. Light, cool, rich soil, in sunny position. Water regularly. Prune in fall, removing old branches. Needs staking but does not twine around supports.

Propagation By semiripe or ripe cuttings in summer; also by layering and air-layering.

Use Easy to cultivate, does well in pots. Very similar to *J. angulare*, which has somewhat larger petals.

111

JASMINUM OFFICINALE L.

Common names Common jasmine, Poet's jessamine.
Order Scrophulariales.
Family Oleaceae.
Origin Southern Asia.

Description Vigorous, branched shrub with twining stems. Deciduous, opposite leaves composed of 5–7 ovate-oblong leaflets, acuminate and sessile, apart from the terminal one which is larger, with a longer point. Highly scented white flowers with a short corolline tube and 4–5 oval petals, in terminal or axillary cymes. White flower buds. Black fruit (drupe), but seldom appears in temperate zones.

Flowering period Summer, on branches of the year.

Cultivation Hardy plant which withstands winter cold if grown against a wall or in a sheltered spot. Sunny position, in rich, well-drained soil. Thin out the branches after flowering.

Propagation By semiripe cuttings at end of summer; by seed in fall.

Varieties 'Affine,' bigger flowers; 'Aureum,' pale-streaked leaves.

Use This is the hardiest of white jasmines which also does well in large pots.

112

JASMINUM MESNYI Hance
J. primulinum Hemsl.

Common names
Primrose jasmine,
Japanese jasmine, Yellow
jasmine.
Order Scrophulariales.

Family Oleaceae.
Origin China.

Description   Small tufted shrub that can be grown as a spreading climber. Persistent, opposite leaves composed of 3 almost sessile, oblong-lanceolate leaflets. Numerous large, unscented, solitary, semidouble, yellow, axillary flowers, with 6–10 rounded lobes, sometimes with a darker center.
Flowering period   Spring-summer.
Cultivation   Half-hardy plant that can tolerate average cold. It may partially lose its leaves in winter. Cool, deep, rich, well-drained soil, in a very sunny, sheltered position. Prune floral branches after flowering. Water in summer.
Propagation   By semiripe cuttings in late spring.
Use   Easy to grow. Not known in the wild state, it is probably a species that has been cultivated since ancient times, as is demonstrated by the semidouble corolla, a feature that does not exist in natural species.

113

JASMINUM POLYANTHUM Franch.

Order Scrophulariales.
Family Oleaceae.
Origin China.

Description   Many-branched shrub with graceful twining stems. Persistent leaves, occasionally semideciduous, opposite, composed of 5–7 ovate-lanceolate leaflets. Highly scented, tubular white flowers, with 5 stellate petals, 30–40 to the axillary panicle. The pink-flushed flower buds appear as early as winter.
Flowering period   Freely, in late spring-summer.
Cultivation   Half-hardy plant that in temperate climates only grows well in warm, sheltered spots. In conservatories flowers tend to appear earlier, in winter. Sunny, bright position, in cool, rich, well-drained soil. Hard prune in late fall.
Propagation   By semiripe or hardwood cuttings in late summer.
Use   Easy to grow, in pots as well. The numerous compact flowers are beautiful but last only 2–3 weeks.

114 ASARINA BARCLAIANA Pennell
Maurandya barclaiana Lindl.

Order Scrophulariales.
Family Scrophulariaceae.
Origin Mexico.

Description Perennial herbaceous plant, woody at the base, with graceful stems, climbing by means of leaf stalks. Persistent, cordate, glabrous, ovate-triangular leaves, with a stalk that is longer than the blade. Large, solitary, drooping, long-stalked flowers, purple with white fauces, hairy on the outside, at the upper leaf axils; corolla swollen at the base, bilabiate, the upper lip bilobed and turned back, the lower lip trilobed.
Flowering period Summer.
Cultivation Half-hardy plant that does not tolerate frost. In temperate climates it is grown outside as an annual. Sunny, sheltered position, in manured, well-drained soil. Water freely during growth.
Propagation By cuttings in late summer or late winter; also by seed in late winter, under glass.
Varieties 'Alba,' 'Coccinea,' 'Rosea,' respectively with white, red, and pink flowers; 'Grandiflora,' larger flowers.
Use Grows well in pots and when sown flowers the same year. Adapts to conservatories, where it flowers longer. Provides good cover for walls.

115 RODOCHITON ATROSANGUINEUM (Zucc.) Rothm.
R. volubile Zucc.

Order Scrophulariales.
Family Scrophulariaceae.
Origin Mexico.

Description Fast-growing perennial herbaceous plant, sometimes woody, which climbs by means of leaf stalks. Persistent, alternate, long-stalked leaves, broadly ovate-cordate, acuminate, slightly dentate at margins. Large, drooping, tubular flowers, blackish violet, terminating in 5 lobes, with flaring, bell-shaped, purple calyx.
Flowering period From summer to first frosts.
Cultivation Half-hardy climber that grows in the open at minimum temperatures above 43°–45°F (6°–7°C). In temperate-warm zones it is grown as an annual. Well-drained soil, in sun or half-shade.
Propagation By seed in early spring, flowering the same year.
Use For rapid cover.

116

ASTERANTHERA OVATA (Cav.) Hanst.

Order Scrophulariales.
Family Gesneriaceae.
Origin Chile.

Description In its original regions it is a small shrub 10–14 feet (3–4 m) high, with clinging roots and hairy adventitious stems at the nodes. Persistent, opposite, very small, broadly ovate leaves, with 2–5 obtuse teeth on either side, and silky pubescence. Showy axillary flowers, solitary or in pairs, red, with a long tube and lower lip often streaked yellow.

Flowering period Summer.

Cultivation Hardy plant which lives outside in climates with harsh winters. Cool, rich, preferably slightly acid soil. Partial shade, even facing north.

Propagation By stem cuttings in late summer.

Use Valued for its lovely foliage; an excellent carpeting plant, for covering trunks and horizontal shady surfaces.

117

MITRARIA COCCINEA Cazv.

Order Scrophulariales.
Family Gesneriaceae.
Origin Chile.

Description Small shrub with slender stems. Small, persistent, opposite, ovate, coriaceous, pointed leaves, with a few teeth at the margins and a rounded base; shiny above, blue-green below. Showy, solitary, axillary flowers on long, drooping stalks; violet calyx; long, swollen, red corolline tube, terminating in 5 almost equal lobes; 4 protruding stamens. Fruit (berry) with long, projecting style.

Flowering period Late summer-fall.

Cultivation Half-hardy plant that grows best in conservatories because it does not like a dry atmosphere. Peaty, acid soil with good drainage, in partial shade. Water freely during growth phase.

Propagation By seed in spring; by stem cuttings in summer; by root division under glass.

Use Relatively easy to grow, highly ornamental; also in pots.

Common name Black-eyed Susan vine.
Order Scrophulariales.
Family Acanthaceae.
Origin Tropical regions of southeast Africa.

Description Herbaceous plant, perennial in warm climates, annual in cold zones, more or less woody at base, with twining stems. Opposite, ovate-triangular, cordate leaves, with long winged stalk. Funnel-shaped flowers, enveloped by bracts, slightly asymmetrical, with a indoors but also outside if the temperature does not fall below 41°–45°F (5°–7°C). Bright position, even in full sun, sheltered from the wind, in rich, light, well-drained soil. Water more frequently during growth. Outdoors, in the winter, cover the base with dry leaves and where temperatures are extremely low, prune hard before frosts set in. Continue to support the stems and thin out in early spring.
Propagation By seed or air-layering in spring; by cuttings in summer.
Varieties 'Lutea,' yellow flowers; 'Bakeri,' 'Alba' and 'Albiflora,' white flowers; 'Aurantiaca,' orange flowers.
Use Provides rapid cover for trellises. It is a half-hardy plant: in temperate zones, as a patio subject, it is best to renew each year to have stronger plants.

Common names Blue trumpet vine, Clock vine, Sky vine, Skyflower, Bengal clock vine, Blue skyflower.
Order Scrophulariales.

Family Acanthaceae.
Origin Southern Asia.

Description Vigorous, fast-growing shrub with thin, flexible, twining stems. Large, persistent, opposite leaves, ovate-lanceolate, pointed, long-stalked, with roughly dentate-lobate margins. Large funnel-shaped flowers, with a flat 5-lobed limb, blue-violet with yellow or white, bluish-veined fauces, solitary or in loose, axillary racemes.
Flowering period Summer.
Cultivation Delicate plant which lives outside only with minimum temperatures of 54°–59°F (12°–15°C). In temperate-warm zones it is grown either as an annual or a perennial, in which the aerial parts die. Cool, well-drained soil, in bright, sunny position, but shaded and not too hot in summer. Water frequently while growing. Needs support. Shorten tips in late winter to encourage sprouting of side shoots.
Propagation By semiripe cuttings in spring-summer; more difficult by seed, because of high sterility rate.
Variety 'Alba,' white flowers.
Use Not easy to grow, but does well in large pots. Light, airy appearance; very suitable for covering trellises.

120

BIGNONIA CAPREOLATA L.

Doxantha capreolata (L.) Miers, *B. crucigera* L.; *Anistostichus capreolatus* L. *Campsis capreolata* Hort.

Common names
Trumpet flower, Cross vine, Quarter vine.
Order Scrophulariales.
Family Bignoniaceae.

Origin Southeast United States.

Description Fast-growing, compact, vigorous shrub with thin, branching stems; branched tendrils are derived from the transformation of the central leaflet and often bear adhesive disks. Persistent, opposite, coriaceous leaves, composed of 2 stalked, ovate-lanceolate, acuminate leaflets, cordate at base. Large tubular, funnel-shaped, orange-red flowers in inflorescences at the axils of the upper leaves. Drooping, straight fruit (capsule) containing numerous seeds.

Flowering period Late spring, early summer, on branches of the year.

Cultivation Half-hardy plant that does well outside in Mediterranean-type climates; in cooler areas it partially loses its leaves and gets through the winter if planted in sheltered, well-exposed spots. Sunny positions, in rich, well-drained, even slightly clayey soil. Water more frequently while growing because the plant does not thrive in dry ground. Shorten tips at end of winter, especially in older specimens. It is often assailed by parasites.

Propagation By semiripe cuttings in summer; by layering, because it roots easily at nodes; also by seed in spring.

Variety 'Atrosanguinea,' darker flowers and straighter leaves.

Use Easy to grow, even in pots. Because of its luxuriant growth, it is better suited to enclosed areas.

121

MACFADYENA UNGUIS-CATI (L.) A. Gentry

Bignonia unguis-cati L.; *Doxantha unguis-cati* (L.) Reh.; *Bignonia Tweediana* Lindl.

Common name Cat's claw.
Order Scrophulariales.
Family Bigniniaceae.
Origin Argentina.

Description Vigorous, fast-growing, branching shrub with thin, flexible stems; trifid tendrils, without adhesive disks. Persistent, opposite, shiny, ovate-acuminate leaves, truncate at base, composed of 2 leaflets. Large, axillary, stalked, deep yellow flowers, solitary or paired, tubular with 5 broad lobes, the 2 upper ones turned backward. Very long, narrow fruit (capsule).

Flowering period Summer.

Cultivation Half-hardy plant, more delicate than *Bignonia capreolata*; to be grown outside only with minimum temperatures of around 45°–47°F (7°–8°C). It often loses some of its leaves. Sunny position, in cool, rich, well-drained, even slightly clayey soil. Water regularly, less frequently in winter. Shorten tips in late winter to encourage the growth of side shoots.

Propagation By semiripe cuttings in summer; also by seed, layering and air-layering.

Use Easy to grow, also in pots. Masses of beautiful flowers, but only for a few weeks.

122 CAMPSIS RADICANS (L.) Seem.
Bignonia radicans L.; *Tecoma radicans* (L.) Juss.

Common names
Trumpet creeper,
Trumpet honeysuckle,
Trumpet vine.
Order Scrophulariales.
Family Bignoniaceae.

Origin Eastern United States.

Description Vigorous shrub with spreading, branched stems, climbing by means of clinging roots at the nodes on the shaded side. Deciduous, opposite, winged, dentate leaves, composed of 7–11 ovate, acuminate leaflets, pubescent on the underside. Large, short-stalked, funnel-shaped, orange-red flowers with 5 reflex lobes, 4–10 to the terminal inflorescence. Clavate, pendulous fruit (capsule).
Flowering period Summer, on branches of the year.
Cultivation Hardy plant which will withstand intense cold if grown against a well-exposed wall and mulched at the base in winter. Cool, fertile, well-drained, fairly compact soil, in sunny, sheltered position. Hard prune at end of winter. Needs a support during first growth phase.
Propagation By semiripe or herbaceous cuttings, or by seed in spring; by layering in fall.
Varieties 'Atropurpurea,' dark red flowers; 'Flava' and 'Aurea,' yellow flowers.
Use Very suitable for covering pillars and small surfaces; easy to cultivate. The horticultural hybrid *C. x tagliabuana* (*C. radicans x C. grandiflora*), with salmon-red flowers, can also be grown in very alkaline soil.

123 CAMPSIS GRANDIFLORA (Thunb.) K. Schum.
Campsis chinensis (Lam.) Voss; *Bignonia chinensis* Lam.; *Bignonia grandiflora* Thunb.; *Tecoma chinensis* (Lam.) C. Koch; *Tecoma grandiflora* (Thunb.) Loisel.

Common names
Chinese trumpet creeper,
Chinese trumpet vine.
Order Scrophulariales.
Family Bignoniaceae.
Origin China and Japan.

Description Vigorous, fast-growing shrub with spreading stems, with or without clinging roots. Large, deciduous leaves made up of 7–9 ovate-acuminate, serrated leaflets, glabrous on underside. Large, funnel-shaped, orange-red flowers with 5 reflex lobes, in dense, drooping, terminal inflorescences.
Flowering period Late summer and fall.
Cultivation Half-hardy plant that will not tolerate periods of frost. Sunny, sheltered sites, in cool, well-drained soil. Needs supports during first growth phase. Prune last year's branches at end of winter.
Propagation By herbaceous cuttings in spring, hardwood cuttings in late summer; also by layering in fall.
Variety 'Thunbergii,' larger flowers, smaller corolline tube.
Use Easy to cultivate; suitable for covering old trunks, railings, and pergolas.

124 DISTICTIS BUCCINATORIA (DC.) A.H. Gentry

Phaedranthus buccinatorius (DC.) Miers; *Bignonia Cherere* Lindl.

Common names
Mexican blood flower,
Blood trumpet.
Order Scrophulariales.

Family Bignoniaceae.
Origin Mexico.

Description Vigorous small shrub with thin branching tendrils. Persistent, opposite, coriaceous, glabrous, long-stalked leaves, composed of 2–3 ovate leaflets (the middle one often transformed into a tendril),with a blunt or pointed tip.[09] Very big, tubular or funnel-shaped flowers, terminating in 5 broad lobes, red with a corolline tube that is yellow inside, in terminal racemes.
Flowering period Summer.
Cultivation Half-hardy plant that grows outside only in warmer temperate zones. Bright, sheltered position, in cool, well-drained, slightly alkaline soil. Water more frequently in summer. Shorten tips in fall and late winter.
Propagation By cuttings in summer; by layering and air-layering in late spring.
Use Good carpeting plant in warm zones, with masses of flowers. Does not do too well in pots.

125 ECCREMOCARPUS SCABER Ruiz & Pav.

Calampelis scaber D. Don

Common names Glory vine, Chilean glory flower.
Order Scrophulariaceae.
Family Bignoniaceae.
Origin Chile.

Description Fast-growing plant with woody habit in warm climates, herbaceous perennial or annual in colder climates. Deciduous, opposite, bipinnate leaves, the terminal segment transformed into a branched tendril. Swollen, pitcher-shaped flowers with orange-red calyx and corolla, on long stalks supported at the base by a small bract, in showy, dense racemes. Oblong, bivalve, pendulous fruit (capsule), containing many flat, winged black seeds.
Flowering period June-October, continuously.
Cultivation Hardy plant in warmer climates, but does not tolerate frost and can survive the winter in temperate-cold areas only under polythene, after hard pruning. Sunny, warm position, sheltered from wind, in rich, well-drained soil. Water freely during summer. Roots easily and grows rapidly; if sown in early spring, it reaches several meters by the end of June and flowers already in the first year.
Propagation By seed in July-August. To obtain flowers the same year, sow in March under glass, then transplant outside in May.
Varieties 'Aureus,' yellow flowers; 'Roseus,' deep pink flowers; 'Carmineus,' crimson flowers, 'Ruber,' deep red flowers.

126 PANDOREA JASMINOIDES (Cunn.) K. Schum.

Bignonia jasminoides Cunn.; *Tecoma jasminoides* Lindl.

Common name Bower vine
Order Scropulariales.
Family Bignoniaceae.
Origin Australia.

Description Vigorous shrub with thin twining stems, but no tendrils. Persistent, opposite leaves, composed of 5–9 sub-sessile, ovate-lanceolate leaflets, shiny, with entire margins. Large, tubular or funnel-shaped, 5-lobed flowers, white with purple fauces, solitary or in panicles, axillary or terminal.

Flowering period From spring to late summer.

Cultivation Half-hardy plant that does not withstand long periods of frost. Bright position, in rich, well-drained soil; slightly acid soil stimulates growth. Water freely during growth. Prune in fall or end of winter.

Propagation By cuttings in summer; by seed in spring.

Variety 'Alba,' white fauces.

Use Suitable to grow in pots only in early years.

127 PODRANEA RICASOLIANA (Tanfani) T. Sprague

Pandorea ricasoliana (Tanfani) Baill.; *Tecoma mackenii* W. Wats.; *Tecoma ricasoliana* Tanfani

Common name Pink trumpet vine.
Order Scrophulariales.
Family Bignoniaceae.
Origin Southern Africa.

Description Fast-growing shrub with twining stems. Persistent, opposite leaves made up of 7–11 ovate-elliptical, pointed, shiny leaflets. Large, scented, funnel-shaped flowers with a long white corolline tube and 5 broad, purple-pink, violet-veined lobes, in continuous inflorescences.

Flowering period Summer, on branches of the year.

Cultivation Half-hardy plant that needs minimum temperatures of around 45°–47°F (7°–°8 C). Well-drained, fertile soil, in sunny position. Water sparingly during dormancy, freely in dry summers. Needs support. Prune at end of winter.

Propagation By seed in spring; by semiripe cuttings in summer.

Use Good for covering well-exposed arches and pergolas thanks to delicate foliage and continuous flowering.

128 PYROSTEGIA VENUSTA (Ker-Gawl.) Miers

Pyrostegia ignea (Vellozzo) C. Presl; *Bignonia igrea* Vell.; *Bignonia venusta* Ker-Gawl.

Common names Flame vine, Flame flower, Flaming trumpet, Golden-shower.
Order Scrophulariales.

Family Bignoniaceae.
Origin Brazil.

Description Vigorous, fast-growing shrub with thin stems; in regions of origin it is often a weed that reaches a length of 65 feet (20 m). Persistent leaves composed of 2–3 ovate-acuminate leaflets, the middle one transformed into a tendril. Tubular orange flowers, terminating in 5 narrow, pointed, reflex lobes, in showy terminal inflorescences of 15–20 blooms.
Flowering period Spring.
Cultivation Delicate plant that needs temperatures above 57°F (14°C). On patios and in conservatories it may flower as early as winter. Bright position, in fertile, well-drained, slightly alkaline soil. Water less often during dormant period. Needs support.
Propagation By semiripe cuttings in summer; also by layering and air-layering.
Use Mainly as a climber in the conservatory, to be brought outside in summer; can be grown in fairly large pots.

129 TECOMARIA CAPENSIS Spach

Bignonia capensis Thunb.; *Tecoma capensis* (Thunb.) Lindl.

Common name Cape honeysuckle.
Order Scrophulariales.
Family Bignoniaceae.
Origin Southern Africa.

Description Vigorous semiclimbing shrub. Persistent, opposite or 4-whorled leaves composed of 5–9 shiny, ovate-acuminate, dentate leaflets. Large, funnel-shaped, orange-red flowers with 4 lobes, the upper one erect, deeply bilobed, in terminal inflorescences of 6–8 blooms.
Flowering period From late spring to first frosts.
Cultivation Half-hardy plant that lives outside only in climates with mild winters. Bright position, in rich, well-drained soil. Water sparingly during dormancy. Prune at end of winter. Needs support.
Propagation By seed in spring; by hardwood cuttings in summer.
Varieties There are cultivars with yellow and orange flowers.
Use Can be grown in large pots. Dense foliage for carpeting.

130 CANARINA CANARIENSIS DC.
Canarina campanula L.

Common name Canary Island bellflower.
Order Campanulales.
Family Campanulaceae.
Origin Canary Islands.

Description Perennial herbaceous plant with rhizome; many slender stems. Deciduous, stalked, pointed, opposite or 3-whorled blue-green leaves, ovate-triangular at base that is often cordate, with irregularly serrated margins. Large, long-stalked, solitary, drooping, axillary, bell-shaped flowers with 6 reflex lobes, orange or yellow-purple with red veins. Globose, edible fruit (berry).
Flowering period End winter-spring. on branches of the year.
Cultivation Half-hardy climber that does not tolerate intense cold and requires minimum temperatures of 50°F (10°C). Bright, sheltered position, out of direct sun, in rich, light, well-drained soil. Water sparingly in dormant period. Needs support.
Propagation By seed in spring or fall; by division of rhizome in late summer.
Use Can be grown easily in pots. Because of its restricted dimsensions it is very suitable for verandas, ewhere it will even flower in winter.

131 CODONOPSIS CONVOLVULACEA Kurtz
Codonopsis vinciflora Kom.

Order Campanulales.
Family Campanulaceae.
Origin Western China.

Description Perennial herbaceous plant with tuberous roots; slightly branching, paired stems. Deciduous, alternate, ovate-lanceolate leaves, entire or roughly dentate. Large, long-stalked, bell-shaped, violet-blue flowers, with 5 almost flat lobes, solitary or in small groups at branch tips.
Flowering period Summer.
Cultivation Hardy plant that even tolerates frost. Sunny or partially shady positions, in rich, cool, well-drained soil. Needs support or it will climb over other plants.
Propagation By seed in spring or fall; by division of clumps in spring.
Variety 'Alba,' white flowers.
Use Because so compact, it is suitable for growing in pots.

132 MANETTIA INFLATA Sprague
Manettia bicolor Hook. f.

Common names
Brazilian firecracker,
Firecracker vine.
Order Rubiales.
Family Rubiaceae.
Origin South America.

Description Fast-growing perennial herbaceous plant with woody base and twining stems. Persistent, opposite, ovate-oblong leaves. Small, long-stalked, showy flowers with a very long tube terminating in 5 small lobes, red at base and yellow at tip, pubescent, at upper leaf axils.

Flowering period From spring to fall, continuously.

Cultivation Half-hardy plant that cannot withstand temperatures lower than 47°–50°F (8°–10°C); survives outdoors in warm, sheltered zones. Partially shady site, especially in midsummer, in cool, rich, well-drained soil. Water regularly, less in dormant phase. Needs support.

Propagation By semiripe cuttings in summer.

Use Given its compact growth and small size, it is very suitable for conservatories and indoors. Formerly it was distinguished from *M. bicolor*, but today it is considered a single species, with wide variability.

133 RUBIA PEREGRINA L.

Order Rubiales.
Family Rubiaceae.
Origin Mediterranean area.

Description Grass or shrub with rough, sturdy, elastic, tetragonal stems. Persistent, lanceolate, coriaceous, 6-whorled leaves, erect and spreading when young, then reflex; tiny reflex teeth are present on the veins and margins, and also on the angles of the stem. Small, whitish, 4-lobed flowers, in axillary panicles at the branch tips. Shiny black fruit (berry).

Flowering period Late spring.

Cultivation Half-hardy plant for semishade, which tolerates brief periods of intense cold and frost. Fertile but not excessively rich soil; also adapts well to poor, calcareous soils. Water freely in spring and winter in mild climates.

Propagation By seed in fall; by semiripe cuttings in summer.

Use Sometimes grows wild in woodland. It can be cultivated in pots and used for walls and trellises, although it only gives sparse cover. Interesting as an evergreen.

Common name
Japanese honeysuckle.
Order Dipsacales.
Family Caprifoliaceae.
Origin Japan, Korea.

Description   Lianoid, twining shrub with hairy young leaves. Semievergreen, opposite, ovate-oblong leaves, initially pubescent, then glabrous. The flat flowers at the leaf axils are initially white, then yellowish, highly scented, with a long, slender tube and a markedly bilabiate limb. The fruit is a subglobose, shiny black berry.

Flowering period   Early summer, sometimes with a second crop in September.

Cultivation   Hardy plant that roots and propagates easily. It prefers cool climates and dislikes drought, but will adapt to any type of soil, ideally with a little manure. If raised in pots it needs frequent watering, especially in summer.

Propagation   By semiripe cuttings or by layering in summer. The plant readily emits numerous root suckers which are very suitable for propagation.

Varieties   Var. *chinensis*, with flowers that are reddish outside; var. *repens*, with leaves that are often lobate; 'Aureoreticulata,' green and yellow leaves; 'Halliana,' soft-haired buds.

Use   Hardy plant suitable for providing sparse cover for trellises, trunks, pergolas, etc. It is very vigorous and soon runs wild, being found in wet, shady areas and hedges, and liable to persist as a weed even after crops are harvested.

Order Dipsacales.
Family Caprifoliaceae.
Origin Mediterranean basin.

Description   Fairly tangled, lianoid shrub with downy gray young leaves. Evergreen, opposite leaves, dark green above, blue-gray below. On the flowering branches each pair of leaves are fused to form a sort of large collar around the stem. The many flowers at the axils of the last three upper pairs of leaves are yellow-white, flushed pink, especially in bud. The fruit is a shiny orange-red berry, covered with waxy down.

Flowering period   May-July.

Cultivation   Half-hardy plant that will not tolerate prolonged frosts. Easy to cultivate, it requires light, aerated soil, preferably calcareous, with not too much humidity, in a bright position, flowering best in full sun. It can withstand summer drought.

Propagation   By semiripe cuttings in early summer or by root suckers.

Use   Very suitable for walls, trunks, roofs, and so on. It is decorative both as an evergreen and for its flowers. In nature it is a typical constituent of Mediterranean scrubland.

Common name Scarlet trumpet honeysuckle.
Order Dipsacales.
Family Caprifoliaceae.
Origin Horticultural hybrid derived from cross of *L. sempervirens* and *L. hirsuta.*

Description Vigorous shrub with twining stems, thin when young. Deciduous, opposite, ovate-oblong leaves, pubescent blue-green on underside, the upper ones ovate, often fused at the base to form a single blade pierced by the stem. Slightly bilabiate orange flowers with a long, narrow corolline tube covered on the outside by glandular hairs, in dense whorls at the tips of the branches. Red fruit (berry).
Flowering period Spring-summer, on previous year's branches.
Cultivation Half-hardy plant that does not tolerate intense cold, needing a temperature of at least 41°F (5°C). Cool, humus-rich, well-drained soil, with plenty of water during growth. Sunny or partly shady position; the fairly shallow roots must always be in the shade. Hard prune only after a few years to rejuvenate the plant, which tends to lose its leaves at the base.
Propagation By cuttings, layering or air-layering in spring-summer.
Varieties 'Fuchsioides,' 'Planteriensis,' 'Punicea' and 'Youngii,' all very similar to the type; 'Dropmore Scarlet,' more suited than others to cold winters.
Use Also grows well in large pots.

Order Dipsacales
Family Caprifoliaceae.
Origin Horticultural tribrid derived from cross of *L. americana* and *L. sempervirens*.

Description Very fast-growing vigorous shrub with slightly twined stems. Deciduous, opposite, ovate-oblong leaves, blue-green on underside, the upper leaves sessile but not fused. Scented orange flowers, bilabiate with a long corolline tube, in whorls at the tips of the branches.
Flowering period Summer.
Cultivation Hardy plant that grows well outside even in areas with cold winters. Fertile, well-drained, humus-rich soil, in fairly sunny position, with roots in shade. Water regularly, less often during winter. Needs support.
Propagation By semiripe cuttings in summer, or by layering.
Variety 'Gold Flame,' flowers orange-red, yellow inside.
Use Suitable for covering walls.

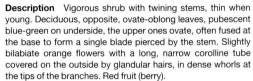

Common names
Common honeysuckle, Woodbine.
Order Dipsacales.
Family Caprifoliaceae.
Origin Western Europe.

Description Shrub with twining stems. Deciduous, elliptical-lanceolate leaves, narrow at base, blue-green on underside, the upper leaves never fused. Scented yellowish flowers, flushed red outside, bilabiate with a long corolline tube, in long terminal inflorescences. Red fruit (berry).

Flowering period Late spring-summer.

Cultivation Hardy plant that does well outside even in harsh winters. Well-drained, manured soil, in fairly sunny position, with roots in shade. Water freely in summer in dry areas.

Propagation By cuttings in summer; also by seed, flowering after several years.

Varieties 'Belgica', red stems and flowers reddish outside; 'Serotina,' purple-red and yellow flowers, lasting until first frosts; 'Graham Thomas,' flowers initially white, then yellow.

Use Suitable for covering trellises and hedges.

Order Dipsacales.
Family Caprifoliaceae.
Origin Horticultural hybrid derived from cross of *L. sempervirens* and *L. tragophylla*.

Description Vigorous, fast-growing shrub with thin twining stems. Deciduous, opposite, ovate-elliptical leaves, downy white on underside, undulate at margins, the upper leaves fused at the base. Unscented orange-yellow flowers, deeply bilabiate, with a long, slender corolline tube, in superposed terminal whorls of 6–12 blooms. Red fruit (berry).

Flowering period Late spring-summer, on previous year's branches.

Cultivation Half-hardy plant that will not tolerate frosts and survives outside only in mild climates. Rich, well-drained, heavy soil, in partly shady, sheltered position. Water frequently and plentifully during growth. Hard prune to reinvigorate the plant which tends to lose its leaves at the base.

Propagation By semiripe cuttings in summer; by layering.

Use Flowers well even if completely in shade.

Order Asterales.
Family Asteraceae.
Origin Chile.

Description Perennial plant with slightly branching stems, often woody at base, which climbs by means of tendrils. Persistent, sessile, oblong-lanceolate leaves, with the middle vein prolonged into a tendril. Very big, solitary, stalked, orange-red capitulum, with numerous central, tubular flowers and 16 peripheral, ligulate and reflex flowers.

Flowering period Summer.

Cultivation Half-hardy plant that grows well outdoors in climates with mild winters. In colder climates it is best raised as an annual, sowing seed in fall. Well-drained, humus-rich soil, in sunny position, but with roots in shade.

Propagation By seed or by suckers in spring; by semiripe cuttings in summer, although rooting is difficult.

Use Suitable as a climber on defoliated tufts, and also grown in pots. The cut flowers last a long time in water.

The drawings show the scales of the flower head and the tendrils. Right: the infructescence and the fruit. The stems of this plant are not much branched and it climbs by means of its tendrils.

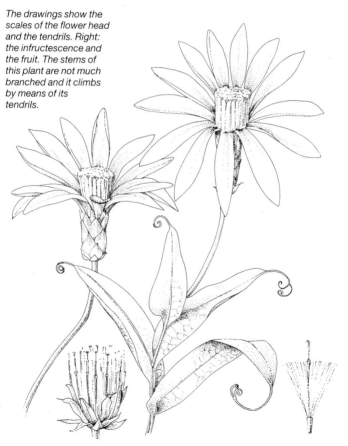

141 DELAIREA CONFUSA (Britton) B. Nord.
Senecio confusus Britton

Common name Mexican flame vine.
Order Asterales.
Family Asteraciae.
Origin Mexico.

Description A shrub in its country of origin but elsewhere a perennial herbaceous plant with a woody base or an annual with twining stems. Persistent, alternate, ovate to cordate-triangular leaves, roughly dentate at margins. Large flowers in heads that are initially orange-red, then turn darker, at leaf axils at tips of branches, in their turn grouped in dense inflorescences.
Flowering period Summer.
Cultivation Half-hardy plant to be grown outside against a wall, in zones with temperatures above 46°–50°F (8°–10°C). Sunny, warm position, in well-drained soil. Water freely during summer. Shorten tips in late winter.
Propagation By semiripe cuttings in summer; by seed in spring.
Use Also grows well in pots. Suitable for covering fences and trellises.

142 GYNURA AURANTIACA (Blume) DC.

Common name Velvet plant.
Order Asterales.
Family Compositae.
Origin Java.

Description Perennial herbaceous plant, often woody at base, a semiclimber, with pubescent stems due to dense purple-violet hairs. Large, persistent, ovate-triangular leaves, entire or with irregularly dentate margins, and dense purple-violet pubescence. Tubular flowers in yellow-orange heads, in short, loose cymes, with a pungent odor that some find disagreeable.
Flowering period Winter.
Cultivation Delicate plant that requires temperatures above 57°F (14°C). Well-drained, humus-rich soil. A bright position in winter helps to give more color to the foliage; provide some shade in summer. Water moderately, less often in winter, but apply to leaves. Needs support. The old leaves lose their color; prune the plant frequently to encourage emission of side shoots.
Propagation By cuttings in spring-summer; roots easily even in water.
Use Very suitable indoors because of compact dimensions; it can stand a dry atmosphere resulting from central heating. It can also be grown as a drooping subject.

143

MONSTERA DELICIOSA Liebm.
Philodendron pertusum Kurnth & Boude

Common names Swiss-cheese plant, Mexican breadfruit.
Order Arales.

Family Araceae.
Origin Mexico.

Description   Perennial plant with partly twining stems, woody at base in tropical climates; it also climbs by means of clinging roots. Very large, persistent, long-stalked, broadly ovate-cordate, shiny, acuminate leaves, entire when young, then with perforations that are transformed into deep incisions. The inflorescence is a spadix, made up of very tiny unisexual flowers, enfolded in a conspicuous yellowish-white spathe. The infrutescence, resembling a pine-cone, is composed of small, edible orange berries that ripen only in the tropics.

Flowering period   Rarely flowers in temperate climates.

Cultivation   A very delicate plant requiring an optimum temperature of about 68°F (20°C). Bright positions favor leaf development, but it is better to provide indirect lighting, and in summer, outside, a site in half-shade. Rich, always cool but well-drained soil. Water the plant, including the leaves, plentifully in summer. Needs a support, wrapped in moss and kept wet.

Propagation   By apical cuttings with at least one leaf, in summer.

Variety   'Borsigiana,' with less deeply incised leaves and less developed clinging roots.

Use   Classic house plant which can also be grown in a temperate greenhouse, where it can climb around trunks, as in its natural surroundings.

144

PHILODENDRON SCANDENS K. Koch & Sello

Common name Heart-leaf philodendron.
Order Arales.
Family Araceae.
Origin Panama.

Description   Vigorous herbaceous perennial, with clinging roots at the nodes; in tropical climates the stems are often woody at the base. Large, persistent, ovate-cordate, acuminate, shiny leaves. Tiny unisexual flowers in a spadix, enfolded by a spathe.

Flowering period   Rarely flowers in temperate climates.

Cultivation   Delicate plant, originally from the tropical forests, needing temperatures of around 59°F (15°C) and high atmospheric humidity. Light, humus-rich, always cool, well-drained soil, in bright position but out of direct sun. Water more frequently in summer, if necessary spraying the leaves. Needs a support, preferably covered with moss, to be kept moist.

Propagation   By apical cuttings in late spring.

Use   It is grown for preference in pots and is a very suitable house plant; also good for trellises and for covering a trunk in surroundings similar to those in a greenhouse.

DIOSCOREA DISCOLOR Hort. Berol. ex Kunth

Common name
Ornamental yam.
Order Dioscoreales.
Family Dioscoreaceae.
Origin South America.

Description Perennial herbaceous plant, tuberous, with twining stems, sometimes woody. Deciduous, ovate-cordate, acuminate leaves, with prominent veins, green with lighter streaks, silvery on upper side, reddish on underside. Tiny greenish-yellow flowers in loose axillary racemes.

Flowering period Rarely flowers in temperate climates.

Cultivation Delicate plant which requires a warm-humid climate with a minimum temperature of around 56°F (13°C). Partly shaded position, in rich, well-drained soil. Water frequently but suspend in dormant period, when the aerial part dies.

Propagation By division of tuber in spring and fall; by seed in spring.

Use Very suitable for pots, also for covering trunks.

TAMUS COMMUNIS L.

Common name Black bryony.
Order Dioscoreales.
Family Dioscoreaceae.
Origin Mediterranean area.

Description Perennial herbaceous plant with twining stems, slightly woody at base. Leaves deciduous, ovate-triangular with cordate base, acuminate, long-stalked, rather shiny. Small, greenish, unisexual flowers (monoecious plant) in axillary racemes, the males elongated, the females short, with 3–5 flowers. Shiny red fruit (berry) which remains on the plant for some time in winter.

Flowering period Spring.

Cultivation Very hardy species which prefers soft, rich soil. Likes half-shade but also grows in full light.

Propagation By seed or clump division.

Use Grows wild in Mediterranean woods and coppices. Very decorative for forming festoons. The berries provide a cheerful note of color in winter.

Common name Prickly false ivy.
Order Dioscoreales.
Family Liliaceae.
Origin Mediterranean area.

Description Vigorous shrub with slender stems and a zigzag habit, furnished with downward-pointing thorns and stipules transformed into tendrils. Leaves persistent, stalked, ovate-triangular, acuminate, cordate, coriaceous, shiny, with thorns on veins and along the margins, sometimes spotted white. Small, scented, white flowers, unisexual (dioecious plant) with 6 reflex tepals, in umbels that in their turn are borne on axillary, terminal racemes. Shiny, pea-sized, coral-red fruit (berry).
Flowering period Early fall.
Cultivation Almost hardy plant, undemanding, able to survive in areas with quite hard winters. Loose, well-drained soil, preferably in sheltered, sunny position, but will also grow in shade.
Propagation By seed or by division of clumps in spring.
Use Commonly grows wild in Mediterranean scrubland. Can be used for covering fences; grows well in pots on balconies and patios.

Opposite: above, the flowers of a male plant, and below, the ripe fruits. Below: detail of a twig with tendrils and thorns.

LAPAGERIA ROSEA Ruiz & Pav.

Common name Chilean bellflower, Copihue.
Order Asparagales.
Family Philesiaceae.
Origin Chile.

Description Vigorous shrub with twining stem. Persistent, alternate, ovate-lanceolate, coriaceous, acuminate, shiny leaves. Large, fleshy, drooping, bell-shaped flowers, solitary or in groups of 2–3, waxy in appearance, deep red with lighter tips; 6 tepals, the 3 inner ones bigger. Yellowish-green edible fruit (berry) containing many seeds with a very short germination period.

Flowering period Late spring-fall.

Cultivation Half-hardy plant which grows outside in a Mediterranean climate with minimum temperatures of 45°–47°F (7°–8°C) in a sheltered site. Well-drained, humus-rich, acid soil. in partial shade. Needs support. Water more freely in summer, including leaves.

Propagation By seed in spring, but flowers only after 3–4 years; by layering in spring or fall.

Varieties 'Albiflora,' white flowers; 'Nash Court,' deep pink flowers; 'Ilsemanni,' larger size; 'Superba,' larger, red flowers.

Use Also grows well in big pots.

GLORIOSA SUPERBA L.

Common names Glory lily, Climbing lily.
Order Liliales.
Family Colchicaceae.
Origin Tropical regions of Asia and Africa.

Description Perennial herbaceous plant with tuberous roots and thin, twining stems. Deciduous, ovate-lanceolate, shiny, sessile leaves, with the middle vein prolonged into a tendril. Very large, showy, solitary, axillary, long-stalked, orange-red flowers, with 6 reflex tepals and markedly undulate margins; long-projecting stamens. Oblong fruit (capsule) containing a hundred or so black seeds.

Flowering period Summer.

Cultivation Half-hardy plant that grows outside in sheltered positions in warm-temperate zones, but is more suited to the conservatory. Sunny site, sheltered from direct sun in summer, in rich, well-drained, loose soil. Water regularly during growth, very often in summer, but suspend after flowering. Needs support.

Propagation By clump division in spring; by seed in late winter in warm surroundings, preferably directly outdoors.

Variety 'Lutea,' yellow flowers.

Use Suitable for large but shallow pots. Keep the tubers in a cool, dry place in winter. Usually flowers in the third year.

Order Liliales.
Family Liliaceae.
Origin Natal.

Description   Perennial herbaceous plant with tuberous roots and graceful, branching stems. Deciduous, lanceolate leaves, the upper ones opposite, the lower ones 3-whorled; the middle vein is prolonged into a short tendril. Drooping, axillary, short-stalked, orange-yellow, bell-shaped flowers, solitary or in small groups, with 6 slightly opened, pointed tepals. Ovoid-oblong fruit (capsule) with numerous seeds.
Flowering period   Summer.
Cultivation   Delicate plant which tolerates minimum temperatures of around 54°F (12°C). Sunny positions, in rich, loose, well-drained soil. Needs support. In winter the aerial part of the plant dies; remove the tubers from the ground and keep them in a cool, dry place.
Propagation   By clump division; by seeds directly outdoors.
Variety   'Keitii', more vigorous.
Use   It grows continuously and does well in pots; can also be raised as a drooping subject indoors.

Common name Chinese-lantern lily.
Order Liliales.
Family Liliaceae.
Origin Natal.

Description   Perennial herbaceous plant with tuberous roots. Deciduous, ovate-lanceolate, shiny, sessile leaves, some with the middle vein prolonged into a tendril. Showy, solitary, long-stalked, drooping, pitcher-shaped orange flowers, at the upper leaf axils.
Flowering period   Summer.
Cultivation   Half-hardy plant that does not tolerate frosts. Sunny, sheltered position, in loose, rich, well-drained soil. Needs support. Suspend watering after flowering.
Propagation   By clump division or by seed in spring.
Use   Because of its small size, it is grown especially in pots. When the plant is dry, remove the tubers and keep them in a cool, dry place.

BOMAREA CALDASII (H.B.K.) Asch. & Graebn.
B. caldasiana Herb.

Order Liliales.
Family Alstromeriaceae.
Origin Colombia and Ecuador.

Description   Perennial herbaceous plant with tuberous roots and twining stems. Ovate-lanceolate, pointed leaves. Large, stalked, drooping, tubular-bell-shaped flowers, made up of 6 reddish yellow or red tepals, the innermost 3 often spotted reddish-brown, in dense umbels.

Flowering period   Summer.

Cultivation   Half-hardy plant, originally from high tropical woodlands; tolerates minimum temperatures of around 41°F (5°C); it is best planted in warm, sheltered spots, mulching the base in winter. Well-drained soil, in bright position. Water freely during dry season, including leaves. Needs staking.

Propagation   By seed or by clump division in spring.

Variety   'Alberic Barber,' creamy flowers.

Use   Much valued for its rich, conspicuous flowers. The *Bomarea* species are strange climbers found through Central and South America. There are some 150 species, most of them wild, growing in tropical forests. Among those cultivated for ornamental purposes are *B. racemosa*, with red flowers, and *B. carderi*, with pale pink flowers.

Right: flower branch and single flower, with characteristic projecting stamens. The flowers are tubular and bell-shaped, in dense umbels.

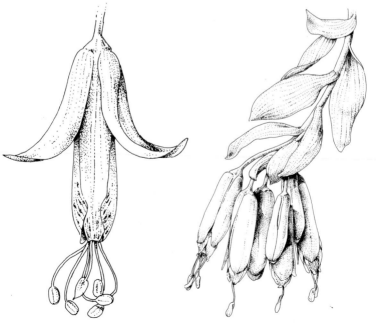

GLOSSARY

Note: the symbol ⟶ which appears after a word within a definition refers to the corresponding main entry in which that word is itself defined.

Achene Dry indehiscent (⟶) fruit that contains a single seed.
Acuminate With a long, slender tip, as of a leaf.
Air layering Method of vegetative propagation, taken from a cut in the stem of a flowering plant to induce root formation.
Alternate Arrangement of leaves alternately at diferent heights on either side of the stem.
Anther Thickened tip of stamen (⟶), often brightly colored, which contains the pollen (⟶).
Aril Outer growth of seed covering, generally fleshy and colored, like the pulp of a fleshy fruit.
Axil Angle formed by a leaf and its stalk on a stem.
Berry Spherical fleshy fruit containing seeds buried in pulp.
Bisexual Said of a perfect flower, i.e. furnished with stamens (⟶) and pistils (⟶).
Bract Modified leaf, often brightly colored, supporting a flower or inflorescence.
Bulbil Small bulb produced above ground by a bulbous plant.
Calyx Outer covering of a flower, formed of sepals (⟶).
Capsule Dry dehiscent (⟶) fruit composed of numerous carpels (⟶).
Carpel Female unit in a flower, containing ovary (⟶), style (⟶), and stigma (⟶).
Clavate Club-shaped, as of a flower organ.
Cordate Heart-shaped, as of a leaf.
Coriaceous Of stiff, leathery consistency.
Corolla Ring of flower petals (⟶), usually brightly colored, protecting the inner organs.
Corymb Flat-topped inflorescence or flower cluster.
Cuneate Wedge-shaped, as of a leaf.
Cutting A piece of stem, root or leaf that is cut off and planted to produce a new plant.
Dehiscent Said of a fruit that opens at maturity to release seeds.
Dentate Toothed, as of a leaf margin.
Digitate With fingerlike sections, as of a leaf.
Dioecious Having male and female organs on separate plants.
Dormancy Phase when a plant is dormant or resting, when growth is slowed down or suspended.
Drupe Pulpy fruit with hard internal shell, usually containing a single seed.
Fauces Narrow part at the mouth of a tubular flower corolla (⟶).
Follicle Dry indehiscent (⟶) fruit in which the carpels (⟶) are separated and open along the margins to release the seeds.
Glabrous Without hairs.
Hermaphrodite Flower provided with male and female reproductive organs.
Indehiscent Said of a fruit that does not open spontaneously at maturity.
Lanceolate Lance-shaped, as of a leaf.
Layering Method of vegetative propagation whereby part of a stem or branch is inserted in the soil until roots form and then cut off to continue as a new plant.
Monoecious Having both male and female organs on the same plant.
Mucronate With a sharp terminal point, as of a leaf.
Opposite Arrangement of leaves, on the same level on opposite sides of the stem.
Ovary Lower part of pistil (⟶) containing the ovules (⟶) later transformed into fruit.

Ovate Of similar length and breadth, slightly broader below, as of a leaf.

Ovule Structure inside the ovary (→), inside which is the female gamete.

Panicle Compound inflorescence, with groups of many flowers on short stalks.

Papilionaceous Butterfly-shaped, as of a corolla (→), with one large outer petal (→), two side petals and two fused inner petals.

Peduncle Stalk, at the tip of which is the receptacle (→) that bears the flower.

Perianth Outer envelope of a flower.

Perigonium Collective parts forming the sterile envelope of the flower, when these are indistinguishable, with no distinction between calyx (→) and corolla (→).

Petiole Leaf stalk.

Pistil Female structure of flower, containing the ovary (→) style (→) and stigma (→).

Pollen Grains produced by the pollen sacs of the anthers (→) which originate the male gametes.

Pruinose Powdery or waxy, as of a fruit or leaf.

Pubescent Covered with tiny soft hairs, as of a leaf.

Raceme Inflorescence consisting of an elongated main axis into which are inserted the peduncles (→) of the single flowers.

Receptacle Terminal expansion of the peduncle (→), into which are inserted the flower parts, i.e. sepals (→), petals (→), stamens (→) and pistils (→).

Reflex Folding backward, as of flower parts.

Rotate Said of an organ such as the corolla (→) when the petals (→) are fused to form a flat disk.

Sepal Transformed leaf lnked to the calyx (→).

Sessile Said of a leaf or flower lacking a petiole (→) or peduncle (→) respectively.

Spadix Inflorescence consisting of a fleshy axis into which are inserted sessile (→) flowers, enfolded by a spathe (→).

Spathe Bract (→) enfolding an inflorescence during or after its development.

Stamen Fertile flower organ that produces pollen (→). The stamens collectively form the androecium.

Stellate In the form of a star, as of a flower.

Stigma Terminal part of style (→), when present, or apical expansion of ovary (→) on which are deposited grains of pollen (→).

Stipule Accessory leaflet, usually in pairs, at base of normal leaf.

Style Filamentous body linking the ovary (→) to the stigma (→).

Tepal Flower segment of perigonium (→), not identifiable as a petal (→) or sepal (→).

Tendril Transformed leaf or stem extension of climbing plant that wraps itself around a support.

Ternate In groups of three, as of leaflets.

Umbel Inflorescence with single peduncles (→) stemming from one point.

Undulate Wavy, as of a leaf margin.

Unisexual Said of a flower that bears only stamens (→) or pistils (→).

Vein Element of vascular tissue forming the framework of a leaf.

Verticil A whorl of three or more leaves or flowers arranged around a point on the axis.

Vexillum Brightly colored element of certain plants designed to attract pollinating animals.

BIBLIOGRAPHY

Bailey, L.H. *The European Garden Flora*, Cambridge University Press, Cambridge, 1986

Beckett, Kenneth A. *Climbing Plants* Timber Press, Portland, 1983

Graf, A.B. *Exotica 3* , Roehrs Co., Rutheford, 1963

Davis, B. *The Gardener's Illustrated Encyclopedia of Climbers and Wall Shrubs*, Viking 1990

Dictionary of Gardening of the Royal Horticultural Society, Oxford University Press, Oxford 1965

Herklots, G. *Flowering Tropical Climbers*, Dawson & Sons Ltd, Folkestone 1976

Hortus Third: A Concise Dictionary of Plants Cultivated in the United States and Canada (compiled by Liberty Hyde Bailey and Ethel Zoe Bailey, revised and expanded by the staff of the Liberty Hyde Bailey Hortorium at Cornell), Macmillan, New York and London, 1976

Krüssmann, G. *Manual of Cultivated Broad-leaved Trees & Shrubs*, vols 1-3, Batsford Ltd, London, 1976-1986

Warren, L.W., Derral, R.H. & Sohmer, S.H. *Manual of the Flowering Plants of Hawaii*, vols 1-2, Bishop Museum, Honolulu, 1990

INDEX OF ENTRIES

Common names are given in roman, Latin names in italic. The numbers are the entry numbers.

PICTURE SOURCES

The photographs in this book have been supplied by the Overseas agency, Milan, Italy.

Photographers and agencies: E. Arnone, Aucante-Nature, D. Brown, E. Banfi, A. Carrara, Hervé Chaumeton, Cordier, Cretti, Explorer, M.P.L. Fogden, C. Galasso, J.P. Hervy, R. Koenig, Lamaison, Lanceau, G.A. Maclean, C. Nardin, Overseas/Maia, Oxford Scientific Films, P. Pilloud, Pollens, R.H.S./Smith, Roguenant, K.B. Sandved, F. Scrimali, H. Schmidbauer, A. Shay, Harry Smith Collection, Smith/Polunin, T.H. Snepher, C. Villarosa, A. Walsh

The drawings are by Guido Orlandi

The publishers apologize for any errors or omissions.